Fathers and Sons

Who Will Reconcile Them?

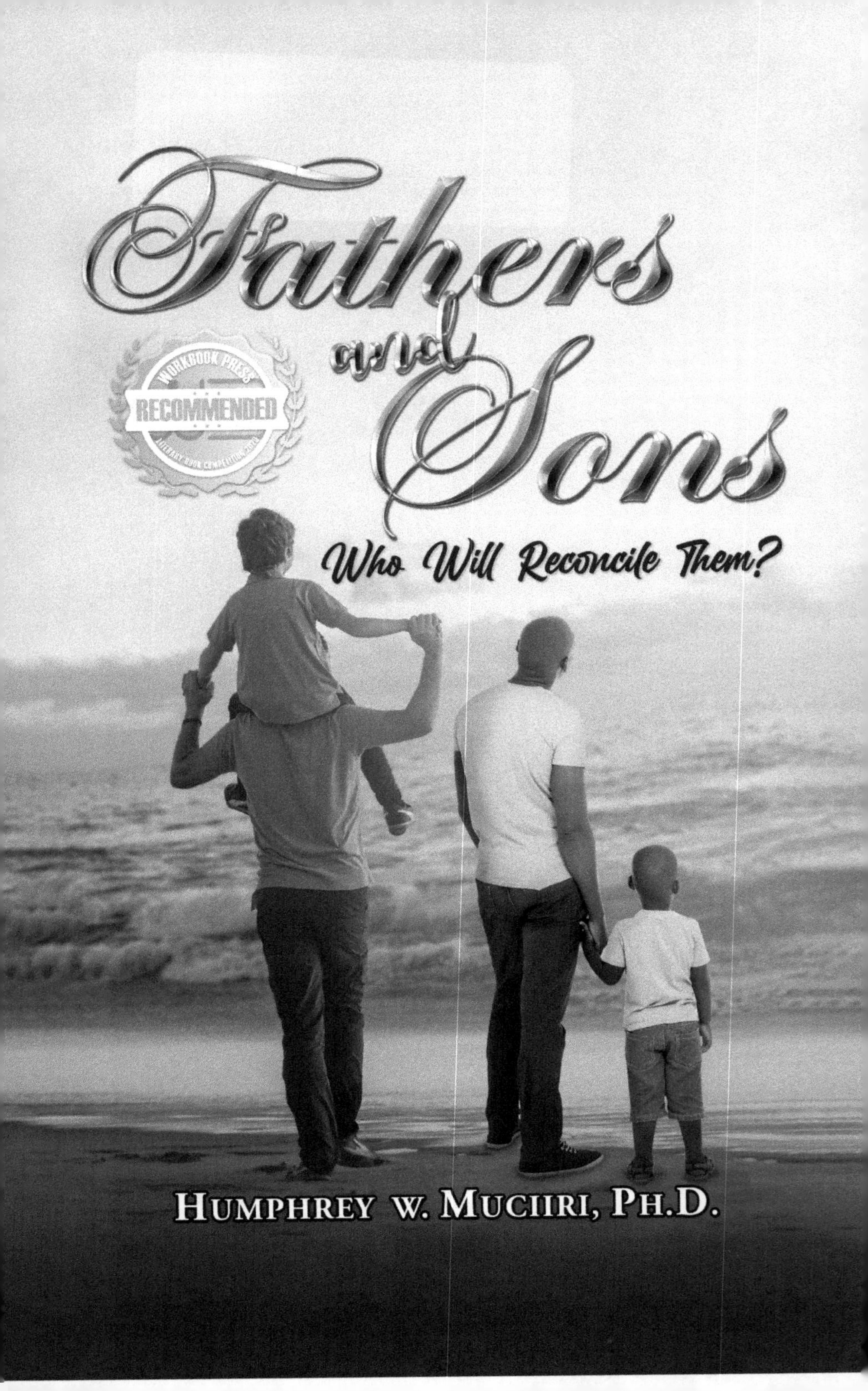

Humphrey W. Muciiri, Ph.D.

Fathers and Sons
Who Will Reconcile Them?

HUMPHREY W. MUCIIRI, PH.D.

WORKBOOK PRESS LLC
187 E Warm Springs Rd,
Suite B285, Las Vegas, NV 89119, USA

Website: https://workbookpress.com/
Hotline: 1-888-818-4856
Email: admin@workbookpress.com

Ordering Information:
Quantity sales. Special discounts are available on quantity purchases by corporations, associations, and others. For details, contact the publisher at the address above.

ISBN-13:   978-1-953839-45-9 (Paperback Version)
                978-1-953839-46-6 (Digital Version)

REV. DATE: 23.12.20

Table of Contents

Dedication

To fathers and sons and all who will read this book,
may God bless you abundantly.

Acknowledgement

I'm grateful to my late father who encouraged and discussed issues with me as a teenage son. When I made mistakes, he did not discipline me without clearly explaining why I needed to be disciplined. My gratitude also goes to the former members of the Grant County, Indiana, Chapter of American Christian Writers Association, who initially read the manuscript and gave me constructive feedback. Many thanks to my wife, Dr. Mary Nyambura Muchiri for her support, constant encouragement, reading the manuscript and making corrections, and also being a sounding board as I wrote the book. May God bless you all and to God be the glory.

Kogi's Visit to his Grandmother

Kogi was born in a rural African village. Major changes were taking place in the country- Independence from the British colonialism was around the corner and a prolonged drought had hit the whole country. The usual green appearance of the countryside had become a monotonous brown color as grass, shrubs, trees, corn, beans, millet, and other crops, were scorched by the hot tropical sun. Majority of the water streams dried up and rivers were reduced to mere rivulets. Herders of domestic animals, such as, cattle, goats, sheep, and pigs wore gloomy faces as they watched their dead animals scattered all over in their farms.

Life seemed hopeless.

Kogi's maternal grandmother lived near a major river. In her little farm along the river bank, she planted drought resistant crops, such as, arrow roots, yams, and bananas trees. She watered them weekly using river water that flowed through a canal dug by her late husband. Her little farm was like an oasis in the middle of a desert.

Kogi's maternal grandmother's health was failing as she grew older. Kogi's mother decided to come to live with her mother, Kogi's grandmother, and help in cooking and watering of her crops. In return, her mother became Kogi's care taker. Kogi's grandmother enjoyed caring for him. She sang nice lullabies to Kogi. She cuddled him, fed him, told him stories, taught him how to walk and speak his vernacular. Kogi became more attached to his grandmother than to his mother.

When Kogi was six years old, he and his mother moved back to their home where his father lived. Kogi's father had built a better and bigger house for the family after the drought had disappeared.

Kogi grew up and loved his maternal grandmother greatly. He looked forward to every Friday evening when his mother gave him food to take to his grandmother. He also helped her do various domestic chores, such as gathering firewood from a nearby forest and fetching water from the nearby river.

One morning at about 8.00 a.m., Kogi went to fetch water from the river for his grandmother. The sky was clear, brilliantly blue, and the sun was shining brightly. The birds chirped as they flew from one tree to another, making Kogi's journey to the river less lonely. Kogi was the first person to arrive at the river that morning. He perched himself on a stone in the middle of the river where water looked cleanest and started to fill his calabash (gourd). No sooner had Kogi half-filled his calabash with water than three boys appeared, each carrying a white plastic container for drawing water.

"Hey, young fellow, give way for us to get some water!" One of the boys barked at Kogi. Before Kogi figured out what was happening, he was pushed aside to fall into the shallow water while clutching to his grandmother's calabash. Kogi was wet, scared, and also furious. He gathered his courage. Suddenly, he grabbed a smooth piece of stone from the river and before he flung it to the face of the bully another boy intervened. The boy grabbed Kogi's hand and ordered his comrades to immediately cease drawing water.

"What is your name?" the boy asked.

"My name is Kogi. And yours?" Kogi inquired.

"Comba," the boy replied.

Comba asked Kogi to fill his calabash with water while the other two boys watched. Meanwhile, Mbaya, the bully, became restless, hissed, shouted insanities and splashed water all over Kogi.

"What is wrong with you, Mbaya?" Comba asked his younger brother. "The river belongs to the community around here. Kogi came earlier than us and has the right to draw water first," Comba admonished his younger brother, Mbaya.

"Go on and draw the water," Comba urged Kogi.

Trembling and speechless, Kogi filled his container with water protected by Comba. After everybody had completed filling their containers with water, they all walked up the hill together heading to their destinations. Kogi arrived at his grandmothers' house first while the other three boys went on to their home.

Kogi did not tell his grandmother about his encounter with the three boys at the river. He pondered over the differences between him, Comba, Mbaya and their third sibling, notably, their behavior and the clothes they wore. "What other differences could there be between them and me?" Kogi wondered.

Kogi's and Mbaya's Backgrounds

Kogi was brought up in the African traditional way of his people. The family lived in a circular thatch hut. The walls were made of red-clay mud placed between wooden sticks tied round wooden poles. The poles formed the perimeter of the hut. After drying, the red-clay walls cracked forming large holes that allowed cold or hot air to get inside the hut. The holes were sealed with a paste made of a mixture of white ash and chalk which after drying, gave the house an outstanding appearance in the neighborhood.

At the center of the hut were three rectangular stones on which Kogi's mother cooked the meals. The evening meals were served when the family members sat round the three cooking stones. The main meals were boiled corn and beans mashed with green vegetables, Githeri, and roasted unripe bananas, ripe bananas, arrow-roots, gruel made from finger-millet, and wild honey.

The rest of the hut was divided into five sections: the parent's bedroom, the girls' bedroom, a store for the cooking pots, and a small multipurpose room near the main door. The goats and the sheep occupied the bigger portion of the hut. Above the central fire place and eight feet above the floor, were planks of wood arranged closely and horizontally, supported by six eight-foot wooden poles that were fixed on the floor to form a kind of a ceiling (Itara). The space above this ceiling was used to store firewood.

Unlike Kogi, Mbaya was brought up in a less African traditional way. Mbaya's father and mother were primary school teachers. Their house was built in stone, had a strong foundation, beautifully plastered walls, and a concrete floor that was kept spotlessly clean. The house had a ceiling, three bedrooms, two baths, a living room, a kitchen, and a store. The roof was made of corrugated iron sheets with aluminum gutters fitted around the house. During the rainy season, the gutters collected water from the roof into a two-thousand-gallon plastic tank that was fixed outside at one corner of the house. It took one month for Mbaya's family to deplete the rain water from the tank.

The kitchen had a fire place fitted with a chimney. Mbaya's mother prepared food on a charcoal stove placed at the fireplace to ensure that smoke moved out of the house. The family's meals consisted of boiled corn and beans, rice with beans, along with green vegetables. These dishes were fried with some cooking oil, onions, and curry powder. Fried wheat bread (Chapati) with a stew of vegetables and some beef was eaten on special occasions, such as Christmas time.

Mbaya and his two brothers were strict adherents of their parents' church denomination. They were not allowed to associate with other boys who did not go to their church. Their parents were afraid that Mbaya and his two brothers would be influenced to eat sugarcane and honey, both of which were used to make an alcoholic traditional beverage. Drinking the traditional alcoholic beverage or touching any of its ingredients was considered sinful by their church denomination.

Mbaya and his brothers were always curious why boys and girls from other families enjoyed playing together, ate sugarcane, honey, and other traditional foods that their parents forbade them to eat.

Mealtime Discussions

One evening, Kogi's family was having a meal. His parents were jovial as they discussed the day's events with Kogi and his siblings.

"How is your grandma, Kogi?" Kubwa, his father asked.

"She is fine and sends greetings to you all" Kogi replied.

"Thank you for the snuff and ripe bananas you brought from her. Incidentally, did you fetch some water for her?" Kogi's father enquired.

"Yes, but…," Kogi replied.

"But what, Kogi?" his mother curiously asked.

"I nearly broke grandmother's calabash at the river," Kogi responded.

"Why would you do that?" his mother queried.

"You see, I was the first to arrive at the river. As I started to fill the calabash with water, three boys appeared. Each boy carried a plastic container for drawing water. One of the boys barked at me, pushed me aside and started to fill his container with water. Comba, the elder of the three boys came to my aid and protected me from the bully. He ordered the bully out of the river and told me to fill my calabash with water. After we had filled our containers with water, we quietly walked up the hill together. I arrived at the grandmother's house first while Mbaya and his other brothers went on to their home," Kogi narrated.

"It is the early bird that catches the worm. You had the right to draw water before all of them. The bully is not only a shame to himself and his parents but also to the community. Who knows what else he will do?" Kubwa commented.

"Do you know that the bully comes from the Zungu's family?" Kogi's mother told her husband.

"What!" Kogi's father exclaimed.

"The bully comes from the arrogant, disdainful, and religious family who despise our way of life." Kogi's mother explained.

Area Chief and the Elders

One month later, Kogi's father, Kubwa, and Mbaya's father, Zungu, met at a meeting that was convened by the Chief, a government administrator of their area. The Chief wanted to solicit some consensus from the community on how to bridge the gap between the traditional ways of doing things and the newly introduced government policies. He enumerated the new government policies concerning the buying and the selling of land, digging of trenches to stop soil erosion, marriage, the introduction of new agricultural cash crops, such as tea and coffee, and how to curb bad behavior among the youth.

Zungu, Mbaya's father, was seated next to the Chief while Kubwa, Kogi's father, sat among the other elders in the crowd. The Chief called one elder after another to give their opinions on how the new government policies agreed or disagreed with their traditions. Many elders knew that the government policies were contrary to their traditions. Nonetheless, they accepted them. Mbaya's father was more vocal in embracing the policies.

"Our traditions are primitive, antiquated, and unchristian. They should be replaced. As a Christian, I don't allow members of my family to follow them." Zungu told the Chief.

The views expressed by Zungu were followed by an incomprehensible murmur among the elders who attended the chief's meeting.

"Are all of your traditions primitive, antiquated, and unchristian?" the chief inquired facing Zungu.

Zungu, along with one group of elders answered "Yes." Another group of elders answered "No".

The Chief was about to end the meeting without a consensus when he noticed a raised hand among the elders.

"You! What do you want to say?" the Chief asked.

"Thank you very much, Chief, for allowing me to express the views that are held by the majority of us who are here today. While the traditional laws are ingrained in our hearts and minds, we have no experience with the new government policies. It is, therefore, imperative for you to have a committee of elders to examine and compare our traditional practices with the new government policies. This will help in knowing the good aspects of both types of laws. The good aspects will be adopted and the bad ones discarded. The process will also facilitate the adaptation of the laws in the community." Kubwa explained.

The Chief was pleased with the views expressed by Kubwa. He appointed Kubwa the chairman of the elders' committee and Zungu, the deputy chairman. He also gave the elders' committee two months to obtain from the community aspects of the new policies that contradicted their traditions and those that could be implemented.

Kogi's Preparation to Begin School

Kogi looked forward to a day when his father would send him to school to learn how to read and write and do math. He was eight years old and many of his age mates were going to school. Kogi looked after sheep, goats, and cows, the merchandise of his father's business. In Kogi's community, boys of six to eight years old were mentored by older boys from the community who knew how to look after goats, cows or sheep. Kogi was fortunate to be mentored by a grade seven boy who went to school and was good at math and English. Kogi's father, a businessman, knew only how to read and write his own name. However, the exposure to the business world made him aware of the benefits of education.

One morning, Kogi accompanied his father to a nearby shopping center. They passed through a thick forest. The ground was damp and the trees formed a canopy over their heads that made it difficult for them to see the sky. The monkeys stared at Kogi and his father. They made squeaking noises as they jumped from tree to tree. The birds chirped and flew over their heads. Kogi was confused and scared. Suddenly, they saw a river ahead of them across which two large wooden logs stretched. Fearful and unable to speak, Kogi followed his father to the edge of the river where the wooden logs were.

"Watch out your steps as you move over these wooden logs, look ahead to see where you are headed, and don't look down to the river," Kubwa admonished his son. As a demonstration, Kubwa crossed the river three times to ensure Kogi understood how to walk over the logs to cross it. Standing on the other side of the river, Kubwa beckoned Kogi to cross over. Timid and sweating profusely, Kogi stepped on the wooden logs, followed his father's instructions and quickly moved to join his father across the river. Kubwa was ecstatic. "You've now passed my test to go to school.

Let's go to the shops. I'll buy the stationery you need and the school uniform for you to start school in two weeks."

Some minutes later, they arrived at the shopping center. There were three rows of shops on either side of the road. Loud music blaired from some shops and huge ads were fixed on the walls of some buildings to display the merchandise. Kogi and his father made a bee line to the restaurant situated in the middle of the shopping center where delicious local foods and beverages were being served. Such foods included, beef stew with chapati (flat disk-shaped fried bread), fish with ugali (ugali is cooked corn meal), rice with chicken, rice with beef stew, githeri (corn and beans cooked together), fish with rice, cooked vegetables, mandazi (type of doughnut), samosas (triangular-shaped pastry filled with a mixture of cooked vegetables, ground beef or chicken and deep fried), tea and sodas. Although it was lunch time when empty seats would have been unavailable, Kogi and his father found two empty ones and sat on them. When the waiter approached, Kubwa ordered and paid for two plates of rice with beef stew and two cups of tea. The food was tasty, spicy, and steaming hot. Kogi was overjoyed to eat out in a restaurant with his father, and, overwhelmed to see so many people eating lunch together.

Across the road and opposite the restaurant was a store atop which were billboards. The billboards advertised various types and sizes of short trousers (short pants), shirts, dresses, salt, stationery, sugar, and Coca Cola products, such as Coke, Sprite, and Fanta. After lunch, Kogi and his father went across the road and entered the store. The store's manager warmly welcomed them. He requested them to sit down on a bench placed near the store's entrance.

"Can I buy you sodas?" the store's manager asked Kubwa.

"Yes, thank you, but what type?" Kubwa asked.

"Any type you want from our store" the store's manager replied.

"Okay, give Kogi a Fanta and a coke for me" Kubwa requested.

As they were having drinks and chatting with the store's manager, Kubwa produced a list of items he needed to purchase from the store. To Kogi's surprise, most of the items were for him that included two pairs of khaki short pants, two khaki shirts, two exercise books, two pencils, an eraser, a pound of sugar, a loaf of bread, and half a pound of salt. Kubwa gave the list of the items to the store's manager, who after perusing, summoned Kogi to a small fitting room in the store.

"Try these pairs of short pants and the shirts and tell me how you feel in them," the store's manager told Kogi.

After fumbling with the clothes for a while, Kogi found that the first lot of pants and shirts was too large for him. The second lot was too tight on him but the third lot was a perfect fit. Kogi's father and the store's manager congratulated Kogi on his new uniform. Then the store's manager gathered all the items, called Kubwa to see every item as he packed them in two separate paper bags. Kubwa got the invoice for the items and paid for them in cash.

Kogi Goes to School

Kogi walked barefoot two miles away to start school for the first time. Wearing his new khaki uniform and carrying the books his father bought, Kogi arrived at school much earlier than other students. In the middle of the school compound was a long rectangular building whose walls were well plastered both on the inside and outside. The roof was made of corrugated iron sheets with gutters to collect the rain water. The building had four classrooms and one office.

"Which classroom should I enter?" Kogi wondered. Before he decided what to do, an office cleaner arrived.

"How are you, young man?" said the school cleaner.

"Fine, thank you," Kogi replied.

"Is this your first day at school?" the cleaner asked.

"Yes," Kogi answered.

"Well, sit on this chair and wait for the headmaster. He will give you the instructions about what to do next," the school cleaner instructed Kogi. A few minutes later, the headmaster came in.

"How are you, young man?" asked the headmaster.

As a sign of respect to the headmaster, Kogi stood up and replied, "I'm very fine sir."

"What is your name?" the headmaster asked.

"My name is Kogi, sir," he answered.

"And your father's name?" the headmaster asked.

"My father's name is Kubwa" Kogi replied.

"So, you are Kogi son of Kubwa?" the headmaster asked as he wrote down the names.

"Yes sir" Kogi replied.

"From now on your official name will be Kogi Kubwa. Leave your books in my office and follow me," the headmaster said.

The headmaster led Kogi Kubwa to a large courtyard outside his office. The courtyard had neatly trimmed grass. The school classroom doors faced the courtyard, and, in front of each classroom students stood up in lines facing their teachers. The headmaster directed Kogi Kubwa to join the line of the first graders.

"Good morning everybody!" the headmaster shouted.

"Good morning sir!" students and teachers shouted back.

With everyone standing up and facing the flag hoisted in front of them, the headmaster counted one to three. During the third count, the students and the teachers began to sing the national anthem. Kogi Kubwa and his colleagues of the first grade were not able to sing the national anthem since it was sung in a foreign language they had not learned. After the national anthem was sung, the headmaster and the teachers inspected each student present for cleanliness. Any students whose hair looked unkempt or wore dirty clothes, and whose body looked filthy were sent home until the next day. The headmaster reminded everybody the school's motto that "Cleanliness is second to Godliness." The motto must be practiced in all aspects of the school," the headmaster stressed.

Kogi's School and Domestic Adjustments

Kogi, and all of the other grade one students were sent to a classroom which had no chairs or desks for them to use. There was only one chair and a table that were reserved for the teacher. At one end of the classroom was a square patch of dirt that was dry, soft, and spread out evenly. The students sat on the floor and watched the teacher demonstrate how to write numerals one to ten on the patch of dirt using the forefinger. Looking at what the teacher wrote, each student wrote down similar numerals at different parts of the dry patch of dirt. Meanwhile, the teacher went round the class looking at the students' work. When the teacher was satisfied with the students' progress in writing the numerals, he gave them pieces of paper containing numerals one to 100. Every student was required to know how to write down from memory numerals one to twenty before the next class the following day.

After lunch, the teacher demonstrated how to write the alphabets A to Z on the same patch of dry dirt. He slowly shouted each alphabet A to Z. The whole class repeated the names of the alphabets in unison, making it sound like a song. Before the class ended, each student was given a second piece of paper containing all the alphabets. The students were required to write from their memory the first ten of the alphabets before the next class the following day.

"Wow! Wow!" Kogi fondly recalled what he learned from his mentor as they looked after goats. He was pleasantly surprised to see the similarity of what the teacher taught them and what he had learned from his mentor. He took his books from the headmaster's office and went home. He was eager to show his parents what he had learned on the first day of school. He got home at about 4.00 p.m. and hid himself behind a cowshed. Kogi started to do his homework. He got so absorbed in his work that when his father arrived and touched him on the shoulder, he freaked out and involuntarily threw off his pencil and the exercise book.

"Don't panic. It's me," Kogi's father said while smiling broadly.

"You scared me so much, daddy," Kogi replied.

"How was your first day at school and what did you learn?" Kubwa asked Kogi.

"It was good and exciting. I can write numerals one to 80 and alphabets A to R," Kogi answered his father.

"May I see what you wrote?" Kubwa asked his son.

Kogi grabbed his exercise book and showed his father the numerals and the alphabets he had written for his homework. Kubwa was pleased and excited by his son's school work. He called his wife to see it.

"Mama Kogi, come! See Kogi's work after his first day of school," Kubwa told his wife.

Kogi showed his mother his school work. Although Kogi's mother could not read or write, she was pleasantly surprised that Kogi was able to do so much on his first day at school. She hugged him.

As they were having their evening meal, Kogi's mother raised a question to Kubwa, her husband.

"Who will be looking after cows and goats when Kogi is in school?" Kogi's mother asked.

"That is a fair question. How many days in a week will you be in school?" Kubwa asked Kogi.

"Monday to Friday and sometimes on Saturdays," Kogi answered.

"Our next-door neighbor has agreed to feed the cows and the goats at a fee. Milking will be done by us. This arrangement will help Kogi do his school work. Kogi will look after the cows and goats only when he has no school work to do," Kubwa informed his family.

"Thank you very much, mom and dad," Kogi breathed a sigh of relief as he thanked his parents for being so understanding.

Kogi and Kega Collaborate

The class started at 8.00 a.m.

"Good morning class?" the teacher shouted.

All of the ten grade one students stood up and replied, "Good morning sir."

"Raise up your hand if you didn't complete your homework" the teacher ordered.

No hand was raised.

For the homework, each student had to write numerals one to 20 and alphabets A to J from memory.

"Sir, I can write numerals one to 80 and alphabets A to R," Kogi reported.

"And me too," Kega said.

"What about the rest of you, class?" asked the teacher. "Can I see your work?" the teacher demanded.

The teacher was happy that the remaining eight students were able to write numerals one to 50 and alphabets A to M.

"Congratulations to each one of you," the teacher commented.

For the rest of the morning, the teacher taught them how to write names, form words, and how to pronounce them.

The class started again after lunch was over. It was January, a summer month in the tropics. Many students were dozing off in class.

"Stand up! Sit down! Stand up again and stretch yourselves!" the teacher ordered the students. "Go and help yourselves in the toilets (rest rooms), wash your faces in the central wash area and come back to class after ten minutes," the teacher said.

The central wash area was a building behind the classrooms that was divided into two sections. The first section contained toilet facilities for boys, beside which were two basins with tap water for washing hands and faces. The second section had similar arrangements but was for girls.

After break, the students were very attentive. The teacher taught them simple sums of addition and subtraction. One by one, the teacher called the students to the front of the class to do simple sums of addition and subtraction. Many of them got it but a few were strugglers.

Classes ended at 3.00 p.m.

"Am happy to be in this class," Kogi told Kega as they went home. "We have a good teacher," Kogi added.

"And me too especially with you as a friend," Kega replied.

"Do you mind us working together for our homework?" asked Kogi.

"That's a good idea, Kogi. Let's start today," Kega suggested.

"Fine, in that case let's start at our home tonight. My parents will be happy to see you," Kogi said.

Their homes were two miles apart. That evening they went to Kogi's home to do their homework.

"Mom, meet my friend from school. His name is Kega. He

lives two miles away from us. We'll be doing homework together," Kogi informed his mom.

"Welcome. You two boys behave well, obey your teachers and you will do well in your work," Kogi's mother admonished. "Here's food for you two," Kogi's mom told them.

Kogi's mother offered them grilled sweet potatoes along with two mugs of hot tea. In fifteen minutes Kogi and his friend Kega, finished eating the potatoes and drinking tea. They thanked Kogi's mom and went off to do their homework. By 6.45 p.m. that evening, they had finished doing sums of addition and subtraction and could write and remember alphabets A to Z and numerals one to 100. Satisfied with their work, they shook hands, walked to the road to join other travelers. It was still daylight, and, Kogi escorted Kega half-way to his home.

"Good morning class!" the teacher shouted.

"Good morning sir," the class replied in unison.

"Hands up if you finished your homework?" the teacher said.

Two hands shot up, Kogi's and Kega's.

"Kogi, come forward. Can you do the first five sums and write down all the alphabets?" the teacher asked.

"Yes, sir, I can." Excited and confident, Kogi went to the front of the class. Meanwhile, other students gazed at Kogi with amazement while the teacher was doubtful about Kogi's ability to do the sums. Slowly but surely, Kogi did the five sums. The teacher graded the sums and found them correctly done. Finally, Kogi wrote down all the alphabets much faster than he did the sums.

Pleasantly surprised at Kogi's performance, the teacher shouted, "Well done, Kogi!" He patted Kogi at the back and asked the class to clap for him.

Kogi's friend, Kega, came forward to solve the last five sums that remained. Although he took longer than Kogi, he did the sums and wrote all the alphabets correctly. The teacher and the students clapped for him as well. None of the remaining students did all of the sums or wrote all of the alphabets correctly.

During lunch break, many grade one students sought help from Kogi and Kega to finish their previous day's homework. Kogi and Kega obliged and made many friends. Meanwhile, the teacher made arrangements for the students to move to a class with desks, chairs, and a chalkboard. That afternoon, he taught them simple multiplication and division during the math class and issued them with reading and math textbooks. The school term was three months. Before the school closed for the vacation, most of the grade one students were reading and doing their math quite well but Kogi and Kega were doing exceptionally well.

Kogi and Kega Promoted

The second term opened in the month of May the same year. Kogi and Kega arrived at school earlier than other students. Their teacher called both of them to the headmaster's office. With fear and trembling, they entered the office. In the presence of their grade one teacher and a grade two teacher, the headmaster smiled and told them to sit on chairs beside their teachers.

"Because of your great class performance last term, we have promoted both of you to the second grade effective today. We expect you to work hard to catch up with second grade work. Do you accept this promotion?" asked the headmaster.

"Yes, we do," Kogi and Kega replied in unison.

Grade two class started at 8.00 a.m. The teacher introduced Kogi and Kega to the class as new students. He asked the other students to say their names for the benefit of Kogi and Kega. Kogi immediately recognized that Mbaya, who bullied him earlier at the river was in that class. Both were now classmates. Meanwhile, the teacher wrote down ten sums on the chalkboard. The sums consisted of a mixture of addition, subtraction, multiplication, and division. The teacher gave the students twenty minutes to solve the sums and hand in their answers to him. Out of fifteen students, five did all the sums correctly. The teacher congratulated them, lined them up in front of the class and ordered the class to clap for them. Of the remaining ten students, six of them had eight sums correctly done while two others got seven sums correctly done. Kogi and Kega did all the sums incorrectly.

Kogi and Kega were embarrassed. This was their worst performance in math. They approached their teacher for help in math during their lunch hour.

"Are you prepared to work hard to catch up with the other students?" the teacher asked Kogi and Kega.

"Yes, sir," both of them replied.

"Are you prepared to sacrifice half an hour of your lunch time every day?" asked the teacher.

"We will. Even if it means sacrificing the whole lunch hour," Kogi and Kega replied.

"Open your math text books on the page about how to do mixed sums-division, multiplication, addition, and subtraction," the teacher ordered. He explained slowly every step how to do a mixed sum. Kogi and Kega were all ears as they listened to their teacher's explanations.

"Do the first sum from your text book and follow the same steps I've shown you. Will you Kogi?" the teacher asked.

Kogi rose up and went to solve the sum on the chalkboard. He did the addition and the subtraction parts of the sum but got confused about what to do first, multiplication or division. The teacher helped him.

"Kega, come up and do the second sum from your text book," the teacher ordered.

Kega stood up from his seat. Holding up his math text book on his left hand and using his right hand, he started writing the answer to the problem on the chalk board. Like Kogi, he found the multiplication and the division parts of the sum difficult to do.

"Watch out carefully as I demonstrate how to do the multiplication and the division parts of the sum," the teacher alerted Kogi and Kega. The teacher discussed with Kogi and Kega each step as he wrote on the chalkboard. Half an hour before the end of the lunch break, he gave Kogi and Kega two mixed sums as home work.

"Remember! You will explain how you obtained your answers of the two sums tomorrow during lunch hour. You are now dismissed for your lunch," the teacher told Kogi and Kega.

That afternoon, the teacher wanted to know how well each student could read. One of the stories in the grade two reading text book was about a race between the hare and the tortoise. Starting from the front of the class, the teacher asked the first student to read the first two sentences of the story. The second student read the next two sentences. Kogi and Kega each read the following two sentences respectively. It was Mbaya's turn to read the ninth and the tenth sentences. As soon as he stood up to read, Mbaya started to sweat. His lips moved up and down making no audible sound. Finally, he sat down without reading a single sentence. Among the remaining students, three were able to read single words in each sentence but could not read whole sentences. The remaining seven students read their sentences to the satisfaction of the teacher. At the end of the class, the teacher asked Mbaya and the three students that could not read their sentences to remain behind.

"Why were you not able to read your sentences like others in class?" the teacher asked. "You are repeaters and you will not be allowed to repeat the class again," the teacher warned the four students. "Go home and practice reading and be ready to read in class tomorrow afternoon," the teacher ordered.

Sheepishly, Mbaya and the other three students rose up at once, bolted out of the class, and headed to a shopping center on the way to their homes.

"Why should those boys, younger than us, embarrass us so much in class?" Mbaya questioned his companions.

"What can we do to save ourselves from feeling so shameful in front of the whole class?" One of Mbaya's comrades asked.

"We know we aren't stupid. We have spent most of our time in extra-curricular activities in place of school work. Let's resolve to work harder at reading," replied a second of Mbaya's comrades.

"No! No! No! School has become very boring to me and my parents don't care about what I do," shouted a third of Mbaya's comrades.

"Let's teach these clever boys a lesson one of these days. After all, we know more about life than they do," Mbaya commented.

"Yes. They know how to read and write but are ignorant about life in general," one of Mbaya's companions commented.

The following day, the teacher noticed that only twelve students were present in class. "Does any of you know why Mbaya and his colleagues are absent?" asked the teacher. None of the students could answer the question.

Meanwhile, Mbaya came in late looking sickly and could hardly open his eyes.

"What happened to you, Mbaya?" the teacher asked.

"I don't know. I woke up feeling ill. May be I ate something bad. Please, give me permission to go and see the doctor," Mbaya requested his teacher.

"Do you know what happened to your other two colleagues? The teacher asked Mbaya.

"No sir," Mbaya replied.

The teacher gave Mbaya permission to go and see the doctor in a nearby clinic. Mbaya's two colleagues did not turn up that day.

Mbaya and his two colleagues did not come back to school for the rest of the term. But, the remaining students performed admirably in both math and reading.

Kogi and Kega, who worked as a team, were top of the class in spite of their late admission to grade two.

Third School Term

The third and final school term begun in September. The school parade went on well. It included the hoisting of the national flag, singing the national anthem, prayers for the new term, and announcements from the headmaster. As a tradition, the headmaster called the first five top students from each class to congratulate and encourage them to do better in the new term. The bottom five students from each class were also summoned for counseling.

"Come on in," the headmaster told Kega, Kogi, and three other of their classmates. "Sit down on the chairs in front of you. How was your vacation?" asked the headmaster.

"It was great, sir," Kogi and his classmates replied in a chorus.

"What did you do?" the headmaster asked.

"I stayed with my maternal grandmother. I assisted in repairing her barn, drew water for her from the river, and also helped mend her homestead fence. I did a lot of math exercises from my textbook and read short stories from a friend's story book. During the last week, I fed my dad's cows. My dad took us to a movie that was being shown at the local shopping center," Kogi answered.

"Very good!" the headmaster exclaimed.

"And you Kega?" the headmaster asked.

"I spent most of the vacation helping my dad at his store. We sold household items, such as, soap, toothpaste, corn flour, beans, sodas, sugar, tea, clothes and so on. The most exciting time was when we went to buy goods for the store. He drove the truck. Occasionally, he showed me how to drive it. He made me sit in front of him and between his legs. I held the steering wheel and steered on the truck. I felt great. I spent the evenings reading stories and being shown by my dad how to do various calculations relating to the store.

"Wow!" exclaimed the headmaster.

"What about you? Was your vacation eventful?" the headmaster asked the third student.

"Yes sir. The three of us went to a camp in one of the city high schools. We were about one hundred students from different primary schools in the country. The teaching was about how to develop good leadership skills, how to be good scholars, and how to develop good character. Small groups were led by senior high school students who based their talk on biblical stories. It was a great and refreshing time since none of us had been in the city before," said the third students.

"Wonderful! What a productive, instructive, refreshing, and great vacation it was! I'm proud of you all. You are good examples to your class and the whole school," the headmaster told the five grade two students. He presented each student with a present commensurate with the GPA achievement in their class. He also gave the students letters to take to their parents.

Five other students came to see the headmaster in the afternoon. They included Mbaya, his three buddies, and one other student from the same class. They were accompanied by their grade two teacher.

The teacher explained to the headmaster that one of the five students had been admitted to a hospital and could not attend school. That student was asked to go, work to catch up with other students in class.

"You four have been absent from your class for one and half

months. What happened?" the headmaster asked.

"We became ill with malaria,"Mbaya answered.

"Were you admitted in a hospital? The headmaster asked.

"No, but we were given drugs that were ineffective," Mbaya replied.

"What did you do to get well?" the headmaster curiously asked Mbaya and his colleagues.

"We got herbal medicine from an herbalist who instructed us to drink it for twenty-five days. Although we got well, we were weak to come to school," Mbaya explained on behalf of his colleagues.

"Do you have any documents to support what you have told us?" the headmaster enquired.

"No sir because the herbalist doesn't read or write," Mbaya told the headmaster.

"Look, the four of you are repeaters. You have no other chance in this class. You must do well this term. Your teacher is willing to help you catch up with work on condition that you cooperate with him. Do you understand?" the headmaster asked.

"Yes, we do," they replied.

"I'm giving each one of you a letter to take to your parents. Your parents will give you a written reply to bring to me before the end of the month," the headmaster ordered the students.

Mbaya and his colleagues went back to their class. They found their classmates reading and doing math effortlessly. To help Mbaya and his colleagues catch up with their class work, the teacher used two methods. First, he asked Mbaya and his colleagues to come half an hour earlier before classes started. The teacher volunteered to help them in reading and math. Second, the teacher arranged the class such that the smartest students helped the less smart ones in math and reading.

Kogi was partnered with Mbaya and one of his friends while Kega was partnered with the other two of Mbaya's friends.

"Hey, we've met before?" Mbaya asked Kogi as they were preparing to read a story from the text book.

"I think so," replied Kogi.

Kogi read a sentence from the class text book and asked Mbaya to read it after him. He stuttered as he read the sentence but finally finished reading it. Mbaya's friend skipped some words as he read the sentence but finished reading all the same.

The following morning before class started, Mbaya and his friend met their teacher for half an hour.

"How did you get along with Kogi for your reading yesterday?" the teacher asked.

"It was good and hope to do better today," replied Mbaya.

"What about you?" the teacher asked Mbaya's friend.

"I didn't read very well but hope to do better in future," Mbaya's friend replied.

"Remember, hard work pays and practice makes perfect," the teacher admonished. "During this half hour, open the page on mixed sums and do the first two problems," the teacher instructed.

After 20 minutes, the teacher graded Mbaya's and his friend's math work.

"Well done both of you. You did the sums correctly. Keep it up," the teacher said.

Physical Attack on Kogi

It was around 5.30 p.m. in the afternoon. Kogi, Mbaya, Kega and some of their classmates were walking home after school. They talked animatedly to one another as comrades. Suddenly, Mbaya changed his behavior. He ordered that the younger boys, namely, Kogi, Kega and others must respect the older boys in their class.

"What do you mean?" Kogi asked Mbaya.

"You and your ilk will be carrying our books when we leave school every day. You will also buy us two packets of candies every week. In return, we will protect you from other bullies at school," Mbaya demanded.

"But we have been helping you in your reading and math at school?" Kogi told Mbaya.

"That's not enough!" Mbaya replied abusively.

"We have nothing els…" Kogi had started to talk.

Before Kogi finished talking, Mbaya and his colleagues pounced on Kogi, Kega, and their other younger comrades. They tore Kogi's books and shirt as they ransacked his pockets. As Mbaya and Kogi wrestled on the ground, Kogi's leg was seriously injured, leaving Kogi helpless on the ground with his leg bleeding. Mbaya and his colleagues ran away and vanished into a nearby forest. The other boys, including Kega, ran away and left Kogi helpless lying on the ground. Feeling much pain, Kogi collected himself, limped along, and got home just before dark.

"Why are you so late and limping?" Kubwa asked his son in disbelief since Kogi was always on time from school.

"I was attacked by some of my classmates. Mbaya knocked

me down, and, as I struggled with him, I was injured. He tore my books and shirt as well," Kogi told his dad.

"What made him do this?" Kubwa asked his son Kogi.

"Mbaya and his colleagues were forcing us to carry their books and buy them candies. This was going to be the price for protection by them from other bullies at school. When we refused, they attacked us. Kega and other boys were able to run away as I struggled with Mbaya. Mbaya and his comrades vanished into the nearby forest and left me bleeding," Kogi narrated to his father.

"This is a very serious matter. Remember what happened to you when you were drawing water for your grandmother?" Kubwa reminded his son, Kogi.

Reactions on Kogi's Injury

Early next morning, Kubwa escorted his son, Kogi, to the hospital. A nurse bandaged Kogi's wound and gave him antibiotics to swallow each time before a meal. It was about three miles to Kogi's school from the hospital. Kubwa and his son wanted to report the injury case to the headmaster. Luckily, one doctor was going home which was next to Kogi's school. He offered to give a ride to Kubwa and his injured son, Kogi.

The school's staff room was lively as some teachers told the headmaster stories about their classes. They were drinking various kinds of beverages that included coffee and tea. Some teachers ate local snacks, such as sweet potatoes, arrowroots, while others ate cookies and biscuits. Suddenly, there was a loud knock at the main staff room door. The headmaster rose up to open the door.

"Oh, oh, what happened to you, Kogi? Is this your dad?" the headmaster exclaimed.

All the teachers were agape to see Kogi in bandages.

"Yes, this is my dad. I was attacked last evening when going home from school," Kogi replied.

"Do you know who attacked you" the headmaster asked.

"Yes, it was Mbaya and his colleagues, all of them my classmates," Kogi added.

Before the headmaster had finished quizzing Kogi about how he was injured, there was another loud knock at the staff room door.

"Good morning, Mr. Zungu? We need some information about your son, Mbaya," the headmaster told Zungu.

"Before you go any further, I got your letter and decided

to come and see you in person about my son, Mbaya," Zungu told the headmaster. As Zungu looked around the room, he saw Kubwa and Kogi.

"What brought you here Mr. Kubwa? I thought you should be with the Chief discussing the agenda for our meeting in a week's time?" Zungu asked Kubwa.

Before Kubwa could answer Zungu's question, the headmaster interjected.

"I'm happy both of you, including Kogi, are here since we have a serious matter to discuss," the head master told them.

"Mr. Headmaster, you sent me a letter saying that Mbaya, my son, was absent from school for one and half months. This can't be so. Every one of those days he reported to me that he had attended school. He cannot lie and has never lied to me. He has been brought up strictly as a Christian," Zungu told his audience.

"Okay, Mr. Zungu. We shall soon find out the truth," the headmaster commented.

Mbaya was summoned to the teachers' staff room. On arrival, he was shocked to see his father, Kogi's father, and Kogi as well.

"Do you see these people here?" the headmaster asked Mbaya.

"Yes, sir," Mbaya answered.

"I will ask you some questions for which I need your answers in the presence of everyone here," the headmaster told Mbaya.

"Were you absent from school last term?" the headmaster asked Mbaya.

"Yes, sir," replied Mbaya.

"For how many months?" the headmaster asked.

"One and half months," Mbaya answered.

"What were the reasons for your absence?" the headmaster asked.

"I said I was ill with malaria," answered Mbaya.

"So far so good," said the headmaster. "But I have a few more questions to ask you," the headmaster said.

"Yesterday when you left school, you went home in whose company?" the headmaster queried.

"With Kogi, Kega and others from my class," Mbaya answered.

"What happened near the forest before you went home?" the headmaster asked.

"We started playing ball and Kogi got hurt in the process," Mbaya tried to explain.

"No sir!" Kogi interjected. "Mbaya and his comrades demanded that we, the younger students, must carry their books from school. Additionally, they asked us to buy them candies every two weeks. They told us that they would protect us from the older school bullies. When I told them we won't do what they wanted they attacked us, beat us up, and Mbaya injured me and tore my clothes. My father took me to the hospital this morning," Kogi narrated.

Mbaya's father went ballistic. He pounced on his son, Mbaya, grabbed him by the neck. Before inflicting harm on him, the headmaster, the teachers, and Kubwa, stopped him. The headmaster dismissed the meeting immediately after fact finding.

"I will report this injury case to the police today for further investigation. But, I will need both of you, Kubwa and Zungu, at the chief's office tomorrow in the morning. Thank you very much. I'll see you later," said the headmaster.

Neighborhood Thugs Exposed

The following day, the headmaster reported Kogi's injury to the police at 8.00 in the morning. To the headmaster's astonishment, two boys from his school were in police custody. They had been caught by a group of neighborhood vigilantes after breaking into a house and stolen three portable radios and other household items. The police officer on duty told the headmaster to report back at 2.00 in the afternoon for more details about the boys in custody. The headmaster went to the chief's office. Kubwa and Zungu arrived at the chief's office promptly at 9.00 a.m. as instructed by the headmaster the previous day. They sat on separate sofas without talking to each other.

"Come on in, gentlemen," the chief beckoned.

"I have been told that a boy named Mbaya bullied and injured another boy as they were going home from school yesterday?" the chief enquired.

"Yes," the headmaster and Kubwa answered.

"I still can't believe that my son, Mbaya is capable of causing trouble to anybody. We have brought him up in a Christian way and he obeys me without question," Zungu said.

"He obeys you without question!" the chief exclaimed. "That may be the problem," the chief commented.

Meanwhile, the chief received a report that Mbaya and other boys were in the police custody because of the previous night's robbery. Although there had been other robberies in the area, nobody had been apprehended by the police. At that juncture, the chief told Kubwa, the elders' chairman, and the vice chairman, Zungu, to call an urgent elders' meeting. The agenda for the meeting was to discuss how to curb bad behavior prevalent among the youth in the neighborhood.

The elders' meeting started at 9.00 o'clock the following morning. The chief said that it was common knowledge that the youth of the area had become uncontrollable. Some had become criminals who broke into peoples' homes and stole various items, especially radios. He emphasized that all criminal elements must be rooted out of the community. Before the chief finished talking, he noticed a forest of hands raised by the elders who were present in the meeting.

"What is your contribution to this matter?" the chief asked Kubwa.

"We already know that Mbaya and another boy are in custody for robbery two nights ago. We need further information from the police to help us deal comprehensively with the whole issue," Kubwa explained.

"It is also alleged that Mbaya is the ring leader of a gang of four or five boys of ages between 13 and 16 years old. They have been terrorizing this area in the last one year," another elder added.

"Yes, he is known to be the ring leader of the criminal gang," a group of elders shouted in a chorus.

"Why wasn't this reported to the police or to me before this meeting?" the chief asked the elders.

"Mbaya comes from a Christian and a well-to-do family. Nobody would have imagined that Mbaya would be involved in criminal activities," the elders replied.

"Mbaya, my son, has been brought up under strict Christian principles. He must have been influenced by bad boys ignorant of the Christian way of life," Zungu said.

As the meeting between the Chief and the village elders went on, policemen brought Mbaya to the meeting. Mbaya looked frail, unkempt, barefoot, and wore jail clothes. He did not want to see his father. When Zungu saw Mbaya, his son, he screamed, became uncontrollable, and suddenly fell to the ground. He seethed and breathed heavily. The policemen put him in their car, drove him to the hospital where he was admitted in the intensive care unit.

Meanwhile, the Chief, and the elders wanted to know what made Mbaya become a bully, a thief, and a gang leader in the community.

"Mbaya, you have been brought up well in a Christian family. Why have you let down yourself, your family, teachers, and the community?" The Chief asked.

With tears flowing from his eyes, Mbaya looked down and didn't answer the Chief's question.

Kubwa, the elders' chairman, asked Mbaya the same question in a different way.

"Mbaya, do you remember when you and your brothers helped my son, Kogi draw some water from the river for his grandmother some time ago? Kubwa asked.

"Yes, Mr. Kubwa," Mbaya replied.

"So, you are good people, isn't that true?" Kubwa asked Mbaya encouragingly. "What changed your good behavior to bad behavior?" Kubwa enquired from Mbaya.

"My upbringing," said Mbaya.

"Can you, please explain what you mean"? Kubwa demanded from Mbaya.

"Yes. I was brought up in a Christian family. My father didn't allow me to mingle with other boys or girls outside our home. I was, as it were, caged in our home. I went to school and back home in time so that my father didn't get angry with me. He told me, as his son, my duty was to obey him without questioning. Yet, I had so many questions in my mind. But, nobody in my family provided me with answers. At school I banded with boys who suffered the same way I did. I became their ring leader. I want to change but I don't know what to do. Please, help me." Mbaya wept uncontrollably as he explained his situation to the Chief and the elders' committee.

"Thank you very much for your candid explanation. We will help you along with the other boys." Kubwa assured Mbaya.

The Chief and the elders were amazed at Kubwa's wisdom in dealing with Mbaya, the gang leader.

Mbaya was taken back in police custody. Meanwhile, the Chief and the elders arrived at a consensus. First, the items stolen or destroyed by the gang of boys were to be returned or paid for by their parents. Secondly, the boys must be sent to a rehabilitation center for behavior correction. Third, ways must be found to keep teenagers occupied when out of school. Fourth, parents were encouraged to engage their teenagers positively by creating good climate for questions and answers in the families. Fifth, all criminal activities in the neighborhood will be reported to the police and the chief without delay.

The Chief was pleased with the outcome of the meeting. He encouraged the elders to speedily implement the policies agreed on during the meeting.

Mbaya's Rehabilitation

Mbaya and his colleagues were housed in three different police cells. They couldn't communicate among themselves. Mbaya was 15 years old but looked like a ten-year old. He was very skinny.

One day, Mbaya and his colleagues were doing their morning chores. They cleaned their cells, the policemen's reception area, and the toilets. When the bell rang, they paraded in front of the national flag as it was being hoisted. Their names were called out and each person answered "Yes sir." The policemen were less harsh and more cordial to Mbaya and his colleagues than they were previously. There was an air of easiness and Mbaya suspected that they were going to be released back to their parents.

But that wasn't to be.

At 9 o'clock in the morning, Mbaya was called out and directed to enter a van whose engine was still running. His colleagues entered other vans that went out of the police station at high speeds. The van that carried Mbaya was the last to leave the police station. Mbaya had heard that there was a maximum-security prison. He imagined that perhaps that was where he and his colleagues were being taken. For nearly three hours, nobody talked to Mbaya because he slept during the whole period.

When the van stopped, Mbaya woke up. In front of him was a huge elaborate gate manned by two tidily dressed guards. Each guard carried an AK-47 rifle hanging on the left shoulder. Atop the gate was a billboard on which was written in big letters "CENTRAL REHABITATION CENTER (CRC)." One guard courteously opened the gate. The second guard asked the driver to stop upon entry to the compound of the center. He got into the van and directed the driver to move on slowly. The compound was immaculately tidy. Grass lawns were tidy with water sprinklers running. The buildings looked clean as though they had been freshly painted. As far as the eye could see, the compound was beautifully kept.

"What a peaceful place. After all, this wasn't to be a maximum security prison I imagined," Mbaya concluded.

The van stopped in front of a huge U-shaped building. The area in the front part of the building was clean and paved. There was also a tall water fountain built in stone and decorated with tiles on its outer part. It resembled a lion that spitted out water to a pool below it. Ten smartly dressed young men of similar age as Mbaya waited. They were accompanied by one staff member.

Arrival at Central Rehab Center (CRC)

As soon as Mbaya stepped out of the van, the staff member approached him smiling broadly. With his hands fully outstretched, he embraced Mbaya and welcomed him to the center.

"Welcome to the Central Rehab Center (CRC) and feel at home," the staff member told Mbaya.

"Thank you sir," Mbaya replied softly.

The staff member introduced Mbaya to the boys who stood by. Each boy said kind words to Mbaya as they hugged him to welcome him in their midst.

"Will you make sure Mbaya is comfortable before supper?" the staff member told the head boy.

"Absolutely sir," replied the head boy.

The head boy took Mbaya to the dormitories. Mbaya was shown his bed and issued with two pairs of grey uniform. He was also given two towels, a pair of black shoes, a pair of sandals, and bathing soap. Immediately, Mbaya went to the bathroom and took a shower. At 6.00 p.m., the head boy took Mbaya to the dining hall. There were about fifty boys who sat according to their age. Mbaya sat among the fifteen year olds, his age mates.

While everyone was talking animatedly, a bell was rung. All the people stood up. A prayer of thanks was said by the head boy. Food was served and everybody started eating their supper. The supper was delicious. It consisted of fried rice, beef stew, and a mixture of various garden vegetables.

After supper, the head boy took Mbaya to meet his counselor. The counselor sat on an executive chair in front of which was a large wooden circular desk. About four feet from the counselor's desk was another area furnished with sofas. There were coffee tables, coffee and tea making appliances, cups and other items arranged neatly around the room. The counselor met Mbaya in this area.

"Good evening?" the counselor said.

"Good evening sir," replied Mbaya.

"I'm glad to meet you. How was your journey?" the counselor asked.

"Long and tiring, but I'm happy it was a safe one," Mbaya replied.

"Will you have a cup of coffee or tea?" the counselor asked.

"Tea, please," Mbaya replied.

As they were having tea, the counselor took out two sets of papers from a folder. He gave one set of papers to Mbaya and remained with another set.

"What you are holding in your hand is the daily program of this center. Study it and the activities scheduled threin. If you have any questions, come back to me," the counselor told Mbaya.

"Thank you, sir," replied Mbaya.

"Remember to be in this office at 8.10 a.m. tomorrow. Okay?" the counselor queried.

"Okay sir," Mbaya replied.

The head boy escorted Mbaya to his dormitory and handed him over to the dormitory prefect - dormitory head boy.

Mbaya's New Life

At 8.10 the following morning, Mbaya was in the counselor's office. He looked confident but unsure of what lay ahead of him.

"How was your first night here at Central Rehab Center (CRC)?" inquired the counselor.

"Comfortable. I feel refreshed," Mbaya replied.

"I'm glad to hear that. I hope you'll enjoy the rest of your stay with us here at CRC," the counselor said.

"I'm hopeful about it," Mbaya answered.

"Well, I understand that you had problems at school. You were a gang leader in your community and you got caught and jailed. True?" the counselor asked.

"It's all true," Mbaya replied.

"What happened?" the counselor inquired.

Mbaya looked down thoughtfully. After a moment of silence, he looked up.

"My parents are staunch followers of a Christian church denomination. In their effort to inculcate the teachings and the beliefs of that denomination, they told me not to mingle or play with boys or girls who did not belong to that denomination. I couldn't ask them any questions. My father told me that my duty was to obey him without questions. When I went to school, my teachers did not address my personal problems. I banded with boys having similar problems and we decided to explore the world around us. That's how I got involved in brawls and became a gang leader. I need help," Mbaya narrated.

"Thank you, Mbaya for being so candid. We'll try to help

you. But, remember you have a big part to play to help us help you. For now, go for a medical examination. Don't forget to come here tomorrow at 8.10 in the morning," the counselor advised Mbaya.

The head boy came for Mbaya and took him away for the medical examination. At the medical clinic, the doctor did a physical examination and drew out some blood from him. The medical report was sent to Mbaya's counselor two days later.

Grade Two at Central Rehab Center

It was time for classes and Mbaya joined grade two. He had lost two terms of classes since his feigned sickness and his jail time. Unlike his previous school, the class was equipped with modern teaching equipment. There were two whiteboards, one in front of the class and another one at the back of the class. Mbaya was one of the twelve students in the class. As soon as the teacher came in, the students stood up.

"Good morning students!" the teacher said.

"Good morning sir!" the students responded.

"We have a new student named Mbaya Zungu. Let's all welcome him," the teacher announced.

One after another, students went and shook Mbaya's hand and said, "Welcome to our class."

In return Mbaya replied, "Thank you."

After Mbaya's welcome, the teacher issued textbooks and exercise books to Mbaya. He gave to the students their graded papers for the previous day's home work. One question in math involved addition, subtraction, division, and multiplication. None of the students had done it correctly.

"Open your math textbook," the teacher asked the students. He wrote the sum on the whiteboard and explained step by step how to solve it. "Do you see how it's done?" the teacher queried. The majority of the students said "yes". To be certain they got it, the teacher wrote a similar sum on the whiteboard for them to solve. He went round the class reviewing it with each student. All, but Mbaya, did the sum correctly.

The teacher gave the rest of the class more math work while

he summoned Mbaya to come forward to his desk.

"What is your problem?" asked the teacher.

"The work is too hard for me," said Mbaya.

"Why?" asked the teacher.

"I missed two terms in grade two," Mbaya replied.

"Well, well… are you willing to work extra hours and weekends to catch up?" the teacher asked.

"Yes," Mbaya replied.

"From today, you will work with one of the best math students in this class. He will guide you through term one and term two math work. Additionally, starting tomorrow you will come to see me at 8.30 a.m., half an hour before the class starts. On Saturdays, you will come to class at 10.00 a.m. I'll be waiting for you. Do you agree?" the teacher asked.

"Yes I do," Mbaya replied enthusiastically.

After class, the teacher asked Stadi, the smartest boy in grade two, along with Mbaya, to remain behind.

"Stadi, will you mind mentoring Mbaya in math?" the teacher asked.

"No. I will be honored and pleased to do it," Stadi replied.

"And you Mbaya, will you cooperate with Stadi to help you catch up in math?" the teacher inquired.

"Yes, sir," Mbaya replied happily.

The teacher turned to Stadi. "Make sure Mbaya understands and is able to do term one, term two, and term three math. Both of you will report to me at 8.30 a.m. daily here in class. Any questions?" the teacher asked.

"No sir," Stadi and Mbaya replied.

Stadi and Mbaya were of the same age and height. They looked like twin brothers. Mbaya was skinnier than Stadi. As they went out of the class for lunch, they planned to meet every day for one hour after lunch, half an after supper, and one hour for each Saturday and Sunday.

Stadi and Mbaya went to the common room after lunch and sat at one corner to avoid interruptions. They opened their math text books from the first page. Mbaya knew how to add, subtract, multiply, and divide. He demonstrated his knowledge of addition, subtraction, multiplication and division by doing selected sums from each page in the first twenty pages of the text book. Stadi was happy with Mbaya's knowledge of math thus far.

After supper, they met again in the common room. Stadi asked Mbaya to solve some selected sums from their text book. The sums involved adding, subtracting, multiplying, and dividing in the same problem. After twenty minutes, Stadi reviewed the answers Mbaya had written. They were all incorrect.

"I see that your additions are correct but not the final answer," Stadi commented.

"Yes. I need to understand how to deal with mixed sums. I missed two terms of class when this section of math was taught,"Mbaya explained to Stadi.

"Oh, oh, what happened?" inquired Stadi.

"In short, I was jailed for being a gang leader in my community. I was also a bully at school. That's why I was brought to this rehab center. I regret it all," Mbaya revealed.

"Thank God! I think it's good for you. I was brought here a year ago for similar reasons. My view of life changed for the better. I used to hold the tail in my class before I came here. I'm now the best student in my class and want to become a computer scientist in the future," Stadi told Mbaya encouragingly.

Stadi's self-disclosure and assurance infused a spirit of optimism and hard work in Mbaya. Though he hadn't told anybody, even his parents, Mbaya wished to be an accountant in a big firm. His dead vision was revived in his mind.

That evening, Stadi asked Mbaya to solve two more of the mixed sums- addition, subtraction, multiplication, and division problems. In twenty minutes, neither Stadi nor Mbaya talked. Mbaya gave his exercise book to Stadi to grade the mixed math problems he had done.

"Wow! Wow!" Stadi exclaimed with a big smile.

"What is it?" Mbaya asked astonishingly.

"You got it! They are all correct!" Stadi exclaimed.

Mbaya was overjoyed.

Stadi and Mbaya hugged, bade each other goodnight, and went to bed in their respective dormitories.

Mbaya's Second Day at CRC

Mbaya couldn't believe it. During breakfast, students from lower level classes mingled freely with students from higher level classes. Young students were not bullied but were mentored by the older students. The atmosphere in the dining room and elsewhere among students was extremely cordial.

After breakfast, Mbaya was required to report at the rehab counselor's office. He had forgotten where the counselor's office was situated. As he stood outside the dining room wondering which way to go, his classmate and mentor, Stadi beckoned him from a far. Mbaya rushed and joined Stadi who directed him to the counselor's office.

Mbaya knocked at the counselor's office door.

"Come on in, Mbaya," the counselor called out. "Have a seat. Would you like to have a cup of tea or coffee?" the counselor asked.

"Nothing for now, thank you because I'm good," Mbaya replied.

"Are you sure?" the counselor said.

"Sure sir. I've just had breakfast," Mbaya assured the counselor.

"In that case, let's get down to business. Your medical examination results are here. Would you like to see them?" the counselor asked.

"No sir. Please, interpret them for me," Mbaya requested.

"The doctor says that you have nothing serious to worry about. However, you have been malnourished. Your medicine will be to eat a balanced diet to ensure you have all the nutrients needed in your body. You are anemic. Continue to eat the food offered in the dining hall. You will have another medical examination after one month," the counselor advised.

"Thank you sir," Mbaya said.

Mbaya went to join Stadi who was waiting outside the counselor's office. At 8.30 a.m., both both went to see their math teacher who waited for them.

"Hi guys! How did you do since you left class yesterday?" the teacher inquired.

"We did fairly well," Stadi and Mbaya replied.

"Would you care to explain what you mean by 'fairly well'"?" the teacher demanded.

"Mbaya has improved immensely in math. In the last exercise, he got all the sums correct. Additionally, his attitude toward work is great," Stadi explained.

"Congratulations to both of you for working so well together. Continue in the same spirit," the teacher commented.

The next math class was at 9.00 a.m. Stadi and Mbaya went and joined the class. They sat away from each other, Stadi on the right and Mbaya on the left with two of their classmates separating them.

"Good morning class!" the teacher shouted.

"Good morning sir!" the students replied while standing.

"Have a seat," the teacher told the students. "This morning, you will do a math test. It consists of twenty sums taken from your textbook where we left yesterday. You have 50 minutes to do it. Any questions?" the teacher said.

No questions were asked. The teacher issued each student with the paper containing math questions. He also gave students five minutes to read through the paper and raise any questions if at all. Since there were no questions asked, the test commenced.

After finishing their test, the students gave their answer papers to the teacher. At 10.00 a.m., the students moved to their next class, namely, reading and English grammar. The English teacher gave Mbaya a warm welcome to the class. She issued him with an English grammar text book and an English story book.

Mbaya's Reading Problems

"This morning we are going to read chapter five of your English story book. Each student will read one paragraph until we finish reading the whole story. Highlight any words or phrases you don't understand. I will explain them after you read the story. Okay?" the teacher said.

"Yes," the class replied in unison.

Out of the twelve students in class, nine of them read their paragraphs very well. Two students had minor problems with pronouncing a few words. Mbaya had the worst time in reading his sentences. He became unsteady and perspired profusely before he started reading. He read one paragraph but the words did not come out clearly because his voice was unsteady. Nonetheless, the teacher clapped for him. He smiled. The teacher asked him to remain behind after class.

"Mbaya, why were you so unsteady that the words you read couldn't be heard?" the teacher asked.

"This is my second year in this class. In my previous school whenever I read something, students laughed at me and I felt embarrassed. The teachers didn't help me either. At home, I lived in fear because I couldn't talk in my father's presence. He said that children were there to be seen but not to be heard," Mbaya narrated to the teacher.

"What a pity!" the teacher exclaimed. "All you need is to have confidence and read. I'll give you a story book to practice reading. Read it aloud to yourself and to a friend as well. Do you have a friend here?" the English teacher inquired.

"Yes, Stadi is my best friend," Mbaya replied.

"Excellent! Work with him. He's a good lad," the English teacher said.

It was break time. Stadi and Mbaya went out together for tea and doughnuts. Stadi looked very concerned about Mbaya's inability to read. Mbaya was embarrassed and unable to talk.

Tea break was over. There were no classes for both Stadi and Mbaya but both of them had half an hour to spare before lunchtime. They went to the common room and sat at one corner away from other students.

"How do you think we can work together to improve your reading ability?" Stadi asked Mbaya.

"I was given an English story book by the English teacher. Would you, please listen as I read and correct my reading errors?" Mbaya begged Stadi.

"Sure, please, start reading," Stadi told Mbaya.

As soon as Mbaya opened the story book to read, his countenance changed. He looked frightened, confused, and was unable to read even a single word. Awe struck at what had happened to his friend, Stadi was dumbfounded. Their silence was interrupted by the lunch time bell, and, without talking to each other, they headed for the dining hall.

Mbaya and Stadi Play Soccer

Sports were held in the afternoon from 2.00 p.m. to 4.00 p.m. Stadi enjoyed playing soccer and Mbaya loved soccer more than any other sport. Prior arrangements had been made for grade two CRC students to play soccer against a visiting grade two class. The best soccer players from each school had been selected for the competition. Stadi and Mbaya were among the best soccer players at CRC.

Before the soccer match begun, each team's captain inspected their team to ensure all players were present. The CRC team wore yellow uniforms. Their goal keeper was dressed in white. The visiting team wore green uniforms and the goal keeper was dressed in red. At 3.00 p.m., the referee blew the whistle and the match commenced. Mbaya played as a left-wing striker and Stadi as a center forward. As soon as Mbaya got the ball, his opponent tackled him. Mbaya dribbled the ball to the right, struck and passed it to Stadi. Stadi in turn struck the ball directly to the opponent's goal. The opponent's goal keeper kicked the ball back toward the CRC's side. The visiting team's strikers were fast and astute ball dribblers. In three occasions, they hit the ball directly at CRC's goal keeper. The CRC's goal keeper deflected the ball away from the goal. Although the CRC's soccer team seemed hard pressed by the visiting team, no goals were scored by either team in the first half of the game.

The second half of the soccer match begun with great enthusiasm from both teams. In the first fifteen minutes, soccer playing was concentrated in the middle of the field. Mbaya snatched the ball from one of the opponents. He dribbled it away from his opponent and hit it. The ball passed between the left goal post and the opponent's goal keeper and got trapped in the net behind the goal keeper. The crowd of spectators rose up shouting "Goal! Goal!" "Goal!" Stadi and other CRC's players ran and grabbed Mbaya, lifted him up and congratulated him on his sterling performance.

The teams changed sides. The referee blew the whistle for the kick off. A visiting team's kicker snatched the ball from Stadi and wriggled through Central Rehab's defenders. He kicked the ball so hard that it passed between the legs of the Central Rehab's goal keeper to hit the net behind him. The crowd rose up with shouts of "Hurraaay! Hurraaay! Goal! Goal!

It was fifteen minutes before the match ended when the second kick off of the second half of the match begun. For five minutes, ball playing was concentrated in the Central Rehab's side of the field. Central Rehab's defenders worked hard to deflect the ball away from their goal keeper. Two minutes before the much ended, a center forward from Central Rehab passed the ball to Mbaya. Mbaya was in an awkward position to score and hit the ball high toward Stadi. Stadi hit the ball with his head. The ball went over the opponent goal keeper's head to the net behind him. It was a goal. There was jubilation and shouts of joy by Central Rehab students and staff. The soccer match ended with a score of two to one in favor of Central Rehab Center.

Both Mbaya and Stadi received congratulations from their teachers and their classmates for the outstanding performance during the soccer match. For once in his short life at Central Rehab Center, Mbaya felt great. Nobody had congratulated him or commended him for anything before he came to Central Rehab Center. The question that lingered in his mind was, "What can I do to enable me read aloud among my classmates and other people without being overcome by debilitating fear?"

The Counselor, the Pastor, and Mbaya

Mbaya reported at the Counselor's office at 8.10 a.m. the following Monday. As soon as he entered the office, the Counselor stood up, hugged him and commended him for his excellent performance at the soccer match the previous week. Mbaya felt embarrassed, looked down and sat on the chair opposite the Counselor.

"What is wrong? Have I offended you by hugging?" the Counselor asked Mbaya.

"No sir, but I did know how to respond to you?" Mbaya replied.

"You should have just smiled and said thank you in appreciation," the counselor advised.

"According to the reports I've received from your teachers, you are doing very well in math, and of course, in games. But not so well in reading. What is your problem?" the counselor asked.

Mbaya looked down pensively.

"I become fearful and stutter every time I stand to read aloud in the presence of my classmates and other people," Mbaya answered.

"Why do you do that?" the counselor asked.

"I don't know but I guess it has to do with my upbringing," Mbaya replied.

"In what way?" the counselor asked.

"In my family, children were not allowed to talk in the presence of grownups," Mbaya told the counselor.

"Aha, that is very insightful, Mbaya," the counselor

commented.

There was a knock at the counselor's office door. The Counselor rushed to open the door. A tall middle-aged man wearing a blue suit and a tie came in. He hugged the counselor, and, both patted each other at the back. They looked very familiar with each other. The counselor introduced the middle- aged man as the Pastor of a nearby Church. He helped CRC's staff and students in their spiritual matters.

"Mbaya, I know you are the son of Mr. Zungu. I would like you to meet my two sons and two daughters at our home on Saturday. Is that okay with you?" the Pastor asked.

"Well, I will need permission from CRC," Mbaya answered.

"That isn't a problem. I will arrange for you to get a permit for Saturday night out," the Counselor told Mbaya.

"In that case, I accept the invitation," Mbaya replied.

"Make sure you are ready at 9.00 a.m. on Saturday and I will pick you up near the dining hall. I will bring you back to CRC on Sunday after lunch," the Pastor told Mbaya.

"Thank you, Pastor, for inviting me to your home," Mbaya replied.

Mbaya had grown to despise Christian families because of his background. Nonetheless, he accepted the Pastor's invitation to find out whether the Pastor treated his children differently from how he was treated by his father. He also wanted to see whether the Pastor's children enjoyed being Christians.

Weekend at Pastor's Home

The Pastor, accompanied by one of his sons picked Mbaya up at 9.00 o'clock on Saturday morning. He drove an immaculately clean four-door sedan car. Mbaya sat in the rear seat while the Pastor and his son sat in the front seats. With a friendly smile, the Pastor's son welcomed Mbaya by extending his hand to greet him. They had travelled for about a mile from Central Rehab Center when the Pastor's son asked his father to stop the car. The Pastor's son moved to the rear seat and sat next to Mbaya.

"Do you like staying at Central Rehab Center?" Caleb, the Pastor's son asked Mbaya.

"Oh yes. It has been a very good experience for me," Mbaya replied.

"Name a few good experiences you have had at the CRC," Caleb asked Mbaya.

"The teachers and the students have been very welcoming and generous. They have made me feel like a member of their family. I'm so grateful to them," Mbaya told Caleb.

"Have you encountered any challenges at CRC Rehab?" Caleb asked.

"Sure," replied Mbaya.

"Such as?" Caleb queried.

"Well, I'm unable to talk and read books aloud in the presence of my classmates or other people. I sweat, get gagged, shake, and become unable to utter any words," Mbaya told Caleb.

"Oh! Oh! Some of my classmates suffer from a similar challenge. Our teacher called it stage fright," Caleb commented.

"Daddy, have you ever suffered from stage fright as a preacher?" Caleb asked his father.

"Oh yes, son. When I preached the first sermon, my whole body shook, I misread my notes, and some members of the congregation thought I was acting my sermon," the Pastor answered his son.

"How did you overcome your stage fright?" Mbaya asked the Pastor.

"That's a great question, Mbaya. My mentor, a senior Pastor noticed my erratic behavior. When the sermon ended, he and I sat down and made a plan. Every Saturday between 11.00 am and noon, we met at church. With my sermon notes ready, my mentor sat in the pews as I preached. He made notes on the good and the bad points concerning my preaching. After 30 minutes, we discussed my performance. This went on for a month after which I developed confidence," the Pastor explained.

"Wow! I thought grown-ups don't get stage fright when speaking to congregations," Caleb commented.

"Me too," Mbaya said.

"You may be correct. But most people not used to addressing groups are likely to experience stage fright," the pastor told Caleb and Mbaya.

Meanwhile, Mbaya noticed that the Pastor had slowed down the car. Ahead of them was a beautiful homestead whose perimeter was surrounded by a manicured cypress hedge. The gate was closed and locked up. The Pastor honked twice, the gate was opened and the car moved in.

"Mbaya! Welcome home," the Pastor and Caleb said in unison.

"Thank you. Am so happy you invited me to your home," Mbaya replied.

As the Pastor was locking up the car in the garage, Caleb led Mbaya to their house.

"Pleased to see you, Mbaya, and feel at home," said Caleb's older brother and two sisters. They escorted him to the living room.

"Thank you for having me in your home," replied Mbaya.

Meanwhile, Caleb's mother and his father, the Pastor came in.

"It is wonderful to see you here in our home. We hope that you will have a refreshing weekend with us. We also know we will be blessed by your presence here," Caleb's mother said.

"Let's stand up, hold our hands together and pray," the Pastor said.

"Oh Lord God from whom all blessings flow, we thank you for all things we enjoy, including the visit of our friend, Mbaya. We pray that he will be a blessing to us and us to him. Bless out time together and all we'll enjoy from your bounty. We pray this in the name of our Lord Jesus Christ. Amen," the Pastor prayed.

We sat on chairs around a rectangular table. Caleb's sisters brought out an assortment of cookies, tea and coffee on a trolley.

"Mbaya, what will you take, tea or coffee?" asked Caleb's sister.

"Tea, please," Mbaya replied.

"Please, help yourself to a cookie of your choice," Caleb requested Mbaya.

"Thank you," Mbaya said as helped himself to a chocolate

cookie.

"Mbaya, how are your parents?" asked Caleb's mother.

"Well…I guess they're okay since I saw them about six months ago," Mbaya answered.

"Are they Christians?" Caleb's brother asked Mbaya.

"Yes," Mbaya said.

"What denomination?" Caleb's sister asked Mbaya.

"I'm not sure of the denomination," Mbaya answered.

Caleb's father interjected.

"Caleb, show Mbaya around the house and the compound before lunch," the Pastor asked his son.

"Yes, dad," Caleb answered.

"Let's go," Caleb beckoned Mbaya.

Caleb and Mbaya went through the kitchen and entered another room in the house.

"Wow! What a tidy room! A working desk in the middle, a shelf with books labeled according to subjects, beautiful pictures on the wall including your girl-friend's, good lighting and a clean floor," Mbaya told Caleb.

"Thanks for your good comments. This is my study room." Caleb told Mbaya.

"You parents are wonderful people for offering you these facilities. I envy you," Mbaya told Caleb.

Caleb and Mbaya moved on to another room.

"This is my bed-room. As you can see I have two beds. One for you tonight and one for me," Caleb informed Mbaya.

"Thank you. I'm impressed," Mbaya said.

"Let's go out into the compound," Caleb said.

'What are those sheds out there?" asked Mbaya.

"For cows and chicken," replied Caleb.

"Do you play ball on the court near the cow sheds?" Mbaya inquired.

"Yes, we play volleyball after work," Caleb answered.

Meanwhile, Caleb and Mbaya were joined by Caleb's older brother and two sisters. It was 12.00 noon and lunch was at 1.00 p.m.

"Hi guys, join us." shouted Caleb's older brother.

"Okay, here we are. What plans do you have?" enquired Caleb from his older brother.

"Let's have a general discussion for Mbaya to know us better," Caleb's brother suggested.

"Oh yes. That sounds great," Mbaya commented.

"Tell us about your family?" Caleb's sister asked Mbaya.

"We are two brothers and two sisters. My father and mother are primary school teachers," said Mbaya.

"How come they sent you to Central Rehab Center?" Caleb's older brother enquired.

Mbaya looked down thoughtfully while Caleb's brother and sisters eagerly waited for an answer.

"My parents didn't send me to CRC. They had no part in it," replied Mbaya.

"Who did it and why?" Caleb's sisters asked.

"It was police and village elders. Sending me to CRC was the best thing that happened to me," Mbaya answered.

"How so?" asked Caleb's older brother.

"I've great teachers and great friends in class and outside class. I'm free to talk and play games," Mbaya replied.

"You mean you had no freedom to talk at your home?" Caleb's sister asked.

"Yes, because I grew under great restrictions from my parents. I couldn't mingle with boys or girls in our village. So, I joined a gang of boys who were school dropouts. We terrorized our village at night by stealing radios and other items which we sold for money," Mbaya explained.

"Oh, my God! So finally you were apprehended and brought to CRC," Caleb's older brother commented.

"Yes, and here we are at your home. Please, tell me how far you've gone in schooling? " Mbaya asked.

"I'm Caleb, 14 years old, in grade six at the primary school. I wannabe a computer engineer when I finish school."

"My name is Marion, 16 years old and a second year in high school. I wannabe a doctor after finishing college."

"Janet is my name, 18 years old, and a senior in high school. I wannabe a social worker after college."

"I am Paul, 20 years old, second year in college. I wannabe an electrical engineer after college."

"And what do you wannabe after school?" Paul asked Mbaya.

"Perhaps an accountant," replied Mbaya.

"How old are you, Mbaya?" asked Paul.

"15 years old and in grade two at CRC," replied Mbaya.

Time was up for lunch and Paul led the group into the house.

Mbaya felt small and inadequate among the Pastors sons and daughters.

"I'm only a grade two student in this group," Mbaya thought to himself.

At the same time, Mbaya's stomach growled. He was hungry.

"How do you feel," Caleb asked Mbaya.

Smiling broadly, Mbaya replied, "Fine, thank you" as they entered the house where delicious lunch was laid on a table. It was buffet lunch, beef stew, mixed vegetables (carrots, spinach, cabbage), rice, and French fries were arranged at one end of the table and fruit salad (a mixture of papaya, mangoes, bananas, melons) at the other end.

"Hold hands," the Pastor said. "I thank you God for food, family, and friends, especially for Mbaya's visit. In Jesus name. Amen."

Directed by Caleb, Mbaya served food for himself first. Caleb was second to serve himself followed by his sisters and brother. The Pastor and his wife served themselves last. They sat round a rectangular table that was covered with a cloth embroidered with blue and pink flowers. It was beautiful. Mbaya sat between the Pastor and Caleb.

"How is your day going?" The Pastor asked Mbaya.

"Very well, Pastor - beyond my expectations," Mbaya replied.

"Example of what is beyond your expectations?" the Pastor asked.

"I envy the freedom your sons and daughters have in speaking to you as parents. Caleb is the best example. The discussions you had as you drove from CRC to here, were like two grownups who respect each other. Your children also know what they wannabe in life. You've given them a good foundation," answered Mbaya.

"Wow! Thank you. You've learned a great deal in a few hours since we came this morning," the Pastor replied.

"Daddy, Mbaya has become my best friend since I met him. We need to help him to read in front of people without stuttering, sweating and feeling fearful," Caleb told his father.

"Yes, Caleb," his father replied.

Meanwhile, as Caleb's mother, brother and sisters ate their lunch, they listened attentively to the discussion between the Pastor, Caleb and Mbaya.

Mbaya was feeling more at ease in this family than ever before. "How would they help me to read and stop stuttering in front of people? I look forward to their help, nonetheless," Mbaya thought to himself.

Lunch was over.

"Let's go to my room," Caleb told Mbaya. As they lay on the beds in Caleb's room for a siesta, Mbaya noticed some books on one of Caleb's shelves that interested him. He rose up and grabbed two small books titled "The Cameleon" and "The Rabbit and the Tortoise" respectively.

"Wow! My grandmother told me stories about the Cameleon and the Rabbit and the Tortoise," Mbaya told Caleb.

"Very interesting," commented Caleb.

Motivated by the urge to tell the story, Mbaya read four pages of the small book about the Cameleon as Caleb listened intently.

"Unbelievable! That is great reading. Congratulations!" Caleb

said.

Mbaya was encouraged by Caleb's comments. He read two pages of the second book about the Rabbit and the Tortoise.

"Am glad I didn't give away those two small books after grade two. From now they are yours. Please, take them, and, remember there're lessons behind those stories" Caleb told Mbaya.

Mbaya was overjoyed. He smiled broadly, hugged Caleb and out they went to see the cows grazing in the compound.

"How many cows do you have?" Mbaya asked.

"Six. Four are black with white spots on their body and two are brown in color," Caleb said. "See, there they are grazing in the compound," Caleb pointed with his forefinger.

As they moved closer to the cows, Mbaya noticed two huge storage sheds. "What is stored in the sheds over there?" asked Mbaya.

"Hay and straw. It feeds the cows during dry seasons," Caleb explained.

"My father had a bull to serve the cows when on heat. How come you don't have a bull to serve these cows?" Mbaya asked.

"We use artificial insemination for our cows. The vet says it is a better way of improving the herd," Caleb explained.

"How much milk do you get per cow per day?" asked Mbaya.

"An average of 30kg (66 pounds) per cow per day," answered Caleb.

"Wow! That is great. My father used to get 18 kg (40 pounds) per cow per day," commented Mbaya. Meanwhile, Mbaya was feeling nostalgic about milking as this was his duty at his home before he went to Central Rehab Center.

"Look! Three cows are heading toward the sheds over there," Mbaya told Caleb.

Looking at his watch, Caleb remarked, "Oh yea. It's time for milking. Let's go there," Caleb informed Mbaya.

The three cows had moved each to a milking station and each ate fodder placed in a trough. Two cows were being milked by hired men. Mbaya wanted to milk the third cow but was not sure Caleb would allow him.

"May I milk this third cow?" Mbaya asked Caleb.

"Are you sure you will be able to milk?" Caleb asked Mbaya incredulously.

"Sure," Mbaya replied.

Mbaya washed his hands as well as the cow's teats. He also smeared some greasy substance to the teats in order not to hurt them while milking. Using hands, he squeezed one teat with his left hand and the other with his right hand. As he squeezed the milk out of the cow's teats, the milk was received in a container in front of him and directly below the cow's udder. It took Mbaya two minutes longer to milk the cow.

"Come and see," Caleb asked Mbaya.

Caleb weighed out the milk from each cow. Each of the hired men's milk weighed exactly 30 kg (66 pounds) per cow.

"Look at the weight of your milk, Mbaya! It's 31 kg (68 pounds). Well done!" shouted Caleb.

The two hired men carried all the milk and stored it in a cooler in the Pastor's main house.

"What an eventful day!" Caleb commented.

"I have thoroughly enjoyed it. Thank you Caleb," Mbaya

said.

Caleb and Mbaya headed to the living room where the rest of Caleb's family waited.

"Why didn't my father bring me up as the Pastor has done to his children? After all, my father is also a Christian and a teacher?" Mbaya thought to himself as they entered the living room.

"Hello, Caleb and Mbaya! I hope you two had a fruitful afternoon?" the Pastor asked.

"Yes, we had a very eventful and enjoyable afternoon," Caleb told his father.

"Good. Hope you'll share with us what you did after supper tonight," the Pastor said.

With everybody seated around the dining table, Caleb's mother told them to join hands for a prayer of thanks to God for food, good health, and fellowship. The prayer ended with a resounding "Amen."

The food smelled delicious. It consisted of grilled chicken, chicken broth, mushed potatoes, mixed vegetables (carrots, cabbage and green beans). The desert consisted of mixed fruits (bananas, papaya, mangoes) and ice cream. Caleb and Mbaya sat next to Caleb's mother. For about 15 minutes, the only noise heard was the clattering of forks, knives, and spoons as everybody was busy eating.

"How many people are for tea and how many are for coffee?" Caleb's mother asked.

Caleb, Mbaya, and the Pastor preferred to drink tea. Caleb's two sisters, his elder brother and mother preferred coffee. As they took their cups of tea and coffee, they moved over to the living room and sat on the sofas.

"As we take our tea or coffee, feel free to share any good or bad experiences of the day to help us learn something from one another," Caleb's mother requested.

"Today, I chaired a church committee meeting to consider how to help needy people who frequent our church grounds on Sundays after services. We formulated a policy for screening them to help know the really needy ones versus the fake ones," the Pastor explained.

"Daddy, what do you mean by "fake ones"? Paul, Caleb's elder brother asked.

"You see Paul, some people are pretenders. They approach church attenders after the service pleading how needy they are for food, bus fare, house rent, or tuition for school. Some of them have been found in bars or expensive restaurants eating and drinking and bragging how rich they are. They take advantage of peoples' generosity," the Pastor narrated.

Shaking his head up and down, Paul said, "I now understand. Thanks Daddy."

"For me, I have a school project. I was given an architectural plan by my professor of a newly designed four bedroomed house. Since my interest is to be an electrical engineer, I was figuring out how I would install electrical wiring system for the house and for house appliances. Am also supposed to calculate how much it will all cost," Paul explained.

"Wow! Wow! What a project!" Paul's Mom and Dad exclaimed.

"Under the direction of Mom, my sister Marion and I helped prepare supper, lay the table and clean the house," Janet, Caleb's older sister explained.

"Thank you very much," all said in unison.

"We had a very eventful afternoon today," said Caleb.

"Please, explain what you did," Marion, Caleb's sister asked.

"I was able to read some books without stuttering and sweating in front of Caleb. This has been my problem since I started school four years ago," explained Mbaya.

"We were having a siesta after lunch today. Mbaya noticed two books I used in grade two – "The Chameleon" and "The Rabbit and the Tortoise" on one of my book shelves. He knew the stories as told by his grandmother. He grabbed the books and read a number of pages without any difficulty," Caleb narrated.

"Praise the Lord! Wonderful! Praise the Lord!" the Pastor exclaimed.

"That isn't all we did," Caleb rose up to tell the family. "As you know, we have always assumed that 30 kg (66 pounds) of milk per day per cow is normal. Caleb milked one of the cows and got 31 kg (68 pounds) today. I think those cows can produce more milk than we know," explained Caleb.

Everybody was agape to hear this piece of news.

"Unbelievable! You mean Mbaya can milk cows?" The Pastor asked incredulously.

"Yes, Pastor. I learned to milk when I was five years old at home," Mbaya said.

"We greatly appreciate you, Mbaya. You have taught us something new about our cows. Please, put your hands together and clap for Mbaya and Caleb. No doubt they had a very eventful and productive day," the Pastor said.

Caleb's mother thanked everybody for making the evening so wonderful and insightful. Overcome by emotions, she hugged Mbaya and thanked him again for what he had done in his short stay with them.

"Caleb, will you say a prayer for us before we disperse to our different rooms? His mother requested.

"Oh God, the creator of the universe, we praise you and adore you. We thank you for our family and our friend, Mbaya. We thank you for giving us a lovely evening and for saving us. Forgive us for the wrong things we did today and renew our relationship with you. Protect us from all harm this night. In Jesus name I pray," Caleb prayed.

And all the people said, "Amen."

As they moved to Caleb's bedroom, Mbaya was questioning himself why his parents, who are Christians, hadn't taught him how to pray.

"Many thanks for your prayer, and, praying for me. You are fortunate to have good and understanding parents," Mbaya told Caleb.

"You are welcome. I hope you and I will have more weekends together in the future, at any rate, while you are still in CRC," replied Caleb.

It was time to go to bed. Caleb slept in his own bed and Mbaya in the visitor's bed.

Sunday morning was the busiest day at Church for Caleb's father, the Pastor. Caleb and Mbaya woke up at 6.00 a.m. and were ready for breakfast at 7.00 a.m.

"Good morning? How was your night?" the Pastor asked.

"Good morning, sir. The night was nice and peaceful," answered Mbaya.

"And we slept like babies," added Caleb.

"Help yourself to some breakfast," the Pastor said.

Breakfast consisted of cornflakes, milk, toasted slices of whole wheat bread, jam and marmalade, margarine, scrambled eggs, bananas, and papaya. Beverages were tea, coffee, and orange juice. There was also hot porridge made of millet.

"This is quite a choice. What shall I have for breakfast?" Mbaya thought to himself. "I'll go for porridge which I haven't had for a while. A toast with margarine and marmalade, a banana, and a cup of tea with milk will do for me," Mbaya planned in his mind. "Oh, I'll have some scrambled eggs as well," he concluded.

The Pastor finished his breakfast at 7.20 a.m. "Would you two be in the car at 7.30 a.m.? I have to be at church by 8.00 a.m.," the Pastor said.

"Yes, Daddy, we will," Caleb replied.

Meanwhile, Caleb's brother, Paul, and the two sisters came for breakfast.

"Hi guys!" shouted Paul to Caleb and Mbaya. "You're the early bird that catches the worm," Paul said.

"Yea, we are going to church with Dad. After church we will take Mbaya back to CRC. He has to prepare for next week's classes," Caleb informed his brother and sisters.

"Oh, we'll miss you, Mbaya. You've been such a blessing to us," Caleb's brother and sisters said in a chorus. Individually they hugged him pleading that he visits them again in the future.

Overcome by emotions, Mbaya responded, "Thank you, thank you."

The Pastor was in the car and honked to call Caleb and Mbaya.

"We are sorry, Daddy. My brother and sisters were bidding

farewell to Mbaya and they delayed us," Caleb informed his father.

"Good, we'll be okay. At 12.15 p.m. when the church activities end, we will go to the Farmer's Choice Restaurant for lunch. After lunch we will take Mbaya back to CRC at 2.00 p.m. What do you think about the plan?" the Pastor asked.

"That is great, Dad. Mbaya will have a chance to see our town as well," Caleb replied.

"I am most grateful for your kindness, Pastor. This will be my first lunch in a restaurant and in a town," Mbaya said.

"You are welcome, Mbaya," the Pastor replied. "We have two church services – the youth service and the adults service that run concurrently from 10.30 a.m. to 11.30 a.m. You and Caleb will attend the youth service. We will meet at the parking lot at 12.15 p.m.," the Pastor said.

As Caleb and Mbaya entered the building where the youth service took place, Mbaya was taken aback to see that boys and girls sat and chatted freely with one another. When the youth service started, boys and girls on the stage played Christian music on guitars, a girl played the piano, another boy played drums, and two girls used shakers as accompaniment to the music. Everybody sang and danced to the music being played.

"Is this behavior Christian? The music is Christian but if my father found me here, he would beat me up. I feel embarrassed though I like it," Mbaya thought to himself.

After 10 minutes of singing and dancing, everybody sat down. A young man appeared holding a sheet of paper.

"Good morning Church?" the young man said.

"Good morning and praise the Lord," the congregation

replied.

"Would all the visitors to this youth service stand up," the young man requested. Ten people stood up, including Mbaya.

The congregation clapped for the visitors.

"You're always welcome to this service and feel at home here. After the service, you will be served with a cup of tea or coffee in the hall. Again feel welcome," the announcer ended.

"Wow, this is a great Church. I am starting to feel at home here. Why doesn't my father's church do church things this way?" Mbaya wondered within himself.

Meanwhile, everybody stood up and the singing went on for ten minutes. The youth pastor went to the pulpit. He said a prayer and everybody sat down on the benches.

"Today, I am going to talk about the lost son, also known as the prodigal son in Luke 15:11- 32, (TEV). The younger son rebelled against his father, requested the share of his inheritance, went away and spent it extravagantly...," the youth pastor narrated.

"I know I rebelled against my father but I didn't ask for my inheritance. Am I any better than this lost son? My father didn't love me. When I confessed to the headmaster of my previous school that I didn't attend school for nearly a whole term, my father grabbed me by my throat. He was restrained from beating me up by the headmaster and others who were present. Shall I ever be reconciled to him?" Mbaya remembered and questioned himself.

The youth service ended at 11.30 a.m.

"Let's go for a cup of tea," Caleb reminded Mbaya. "This is Tara, my girlfriend and also my schoolmate. And this is Mbaya, a friend from CRC," Caleb made the introductions as they drank tea after the service.

"Am glad to meet you," Tara said.

"And me too," replied Mbaya.

Mbaya was enjoying talking with Tara and her friends when Caleb notified him that it was 12.00 noon and both must move to his father's car.

"We must not keep dad waiting as we did this morning after breakfast," Caleb commented.

"See you tomorrow lunchtime Caleb, and bye Mbaya," Tara said.

As the Pastor drove toward the town, Caleb and Mbaya were busy talking between themselves. The Pastor parked the car and led the way to Farmer's Choice Restaurant.

"Welcome to Farmer's Choice Restaurant," a waitress said as she directed them to a table reserved for three people and handed them the menu list. "What will you drink and eat," she asked ready to write down the orders.

"Give each of these young men grilled chicken, seasonal vegetables, French fries, and medium size of Coca Cola drink. For me, bring a grilled chicken sandwich with lettuce and tomatoes plus hot tea," the Pastor ordered.

As they waited for their meals, many people spoke to the Pastor or waved at him as they came in and out of the restaurant. Mbaya was amazed at the Pastor's popularity in town.

"How is your food and drink?" the Pastor asked Mbaya.

"It is very tasty, Pastor. I'm enjoying it. I'm also having an extraordinary experience of eating out in a restaurant for the first time," answered Mbaya.

"You're most welcome," the Pastor replied.

"My food is also very tasty, dad," Caleb informed his father, the Pastor. "Dad, thank you for suggesting Mbaya to visit our family over the weekend. He has become a very good friend," Caleb said.

After lunch, the Pastor drove Mbaya back to CRC in his car after the weekend off.

"Very well, I hope Mbaya has enjoyed the change from CRC to our home over the weekend?" the Pastor asked.

"Yes Pastor. You, Caleb and the rest of the family have shown me how a family ought to live together, respecting one another. Also, today for the first time I saw boys and girls interacting freely at church, singing, dancing together, and talking freely among themselves. Caleb introduced me to his girlfriend, Tara. I've really enjoyed my stay with you. In addition, I'm able to read better," Mbaya narrated.

"That's wonderful, Mbaya. You will always be welcome to our home over the weekends and holidays. Remember, you helped to milk cows and showed us we could get more milk from them. That was a big contribution to our family." The Pastor told Mbaya.

Return to CRC after Weekend—off

At 2.00 p.m., the Pastor arrived at CRC and parked his car near the dining hall.

"How are you all? Welcome back, Mbaya. Many thanks, Pastor for hosting my friend over the weekend. I missed him greatly," Stadi said.

"Thank you, Stadi. We shall miss Mbaya a lot. Make sure he is comfortable here at CRC," the Pastor told Stadi.

Meanwhile, Caleb and Mbaya tearfully hugged as they bade each other goodbye.

"Hey, am glad you are back. I felt so lonely without you, Mbaya," Stadi commented.

"I sure missed your companionship and help," Mbaya told Stadi.

"Did you enjoy your stay at the Pastor's home?" Stadi asked.

"Yes, it was exceptional," replied Mbaya.

"How so and what made it exceptional?" inquired Stadi.

Both Stadi and Mbaya went and sat on a sofa in the common room where they expected no interruptions during their discussions.

"The Pastor is a great man. He and his wife have two sons and two daughters: Caleb is in sixth grade, Paul is second year in College, Janet and Marion are in high school. I felt small and inadequate among them. I wondered why I agreed to come to their home. But, discussions among the parents and the children were so free and meaningful. I had observed this freedom between Caleb and his father as we drove to their home from here. For the first time, I observed what I would call real Christianity in practice. The Pastor's children looked genuine in their actions, in prayer, their interactions, and questions to their parents. Oh, what a contrast to my family!" narrated Mbaya.

"Were you able to connect with Caleb who seems to be our age?" Stadi asked.

"Did you noticed how Caleb and I hugged to say goodbye to each other after they brought me back to CRC?" Mbaya asked.

"Yea, you seemed inseparable," Stadi replied.

"You see Stadi, I experienced some kind of mental freedom with the Pastor and his family. This freedom gave me an unexplainable mental easiness such that when we went to Caleb's study room, I was able to read two small books, 'The Cameleon' and 'The Tortoise and the Rabbit' without stuttering or sweating," Mbaya explained.

"Wow! Incredible!" Stadi exclaimed.

"Yes, it's incredible to me also. Listen as I read two pages from each book. Will you?" Mbaya requested.

Mbaya read two pages from each book in eight minutes without stuttering or sweating.

"Mbaya, this is a great achievement. Congratulations! Let's keep it to ourselves until Monday during the reading class. Our teacher will be impressed," Stadi suggested.

"Yes, yes, thank you. I agree with your suggestion," Mbaya said.

"All of us at CRC are being rehabilitated after being involved in one crime or another. What positive impression do you think you left with the Pastor's family?" Stadi asked.

"I think I gave them a good impression about myself and by extension about CRC. I narrated to them why I was brought to CRC as well as my family's background. This helped connect with them to provide me with the necessary help. Also, because of my experience in milking, I milked one of their cows and produced two pounds more milk than they got before. This was a pleasant surprise to them. They extended more invitations to me on weekends and holidays," Mbaya explained.

"Great! You represented CRC admirably. You also came back a changed person especially concerning your reading proficiency," Stadi commented.

"Many thanks," replied Mbaya.

"By the way, we didn't do our math homework since you were away," Stadi said.

"Let's do it after supper tonight," replied Mbaya.

"Oh, look at the clock. It's 30 minutes before supper. Let's go and wash our faces at our respective dormitories," Stadi suggested.

"Well said. We'll meet in the dining hall at 6.00 p.m.," Mbaya replied.

After supper, Mbaya and Stadi went to the common room to do their homework.

"Mbaya, do you recall that our math teacher didn't give us homework for the weekend?" Stadi asked.

"No," Mbaya replied. "Oh yes. I recall that we did a math test but no homework was given for the weekend," Mbaya said.

"In that case, let's read stories from the story books we have," Stadi suggested.

"Please start and I will read after you. Read from the class text we shall use tomorrow," Mbaya told Stadi.

"Right," Stadi said.

"You were very clear and fluent in your reading," Mbaya commented.

"It's your turn to read," Stadi told Mbaya.

"I'll read two stories from the book our English teacher gave me," Mbaya said.

Mbaya read the stories slowly but fluently and without sweating.

"Very good, you will impress our teacher and the class tomorrow when you read. Keep it up buddy," Stadi commented.

"Thanks for your help and encouragement. I feel more confident than ever before," Mbaya said.

"What an eventful Sunday evening we've had," Stadi commented.

"Sure, it's been wonderful. Let's call it an evening and meet tomorrow at breakfast," Mbaya said. After breakfast the following Monday, Stadi escorted Mbaya to see the counselor at 8.10 a.m. Mbaya knocked at the counselor's office door.

"Come on in," the counselor said. "How are you? It looks like years since we met. Have a seat. How was your weekend with the Pastor? The counselor inquired.

"It was great. My time with the Pastor and his family was very fruitful," replied Mbaya.

"What made it great?" the counselor asked.

"I saw another side of Christianity I didn't know. The Pastor's children were respectful and free to discuss and ask questions from the parents. Caleb, their youngest son and about my age became a very close friend. Through him and the rest of the family, my reading problem seems to have disappeared," Mbaya explained.

"Really? This is good news, Mbaya," the counselor said in disbelief.

"Moreover, Caleb and I went to a youth church service on Sunday. For the first time I witnessed boys and girls working together in singing, reading the Bible, and praying. Caleb introduced me to his girlfriend, Tara. This kind of behavior isn't possible in my parent's church where I grew up," Mbaya said.

"This is amazing! I'm happy that your visit with the Pastor was beneficial, insightful, and transformational. Thank you very much for your detailed explanations," the counselor said.

"I'm grateful to you sir, for organizing my visit to the Pastor's home," Mbaya told the counselor.

"You are welcome. By the way, your progress since you came to CRC is good. Your reading improvement will make it even better. Remember, class two finals are in December, two months from today. I'll see you tomorrow at 8.10 a.m. Have a fruitful day," the counselor told Mbaya.

Mbaya joined his friend Stadi who waited in the common room and both headed to their English class starting at 9.00 a.m. Mbaya carried two reading texts: class two English reader and a story book his teacher gave him.

"Good morning class!" the English teacher said.

"Good morning madam!" the class replied.

"Today will be unusual. I want you to share a story you've read about or been told by a friend or a relative. What did you learn from it? Two students will share their stories in each class until all are done. Okay?" the teacher said.

"Yes madam," the students shouted back in agreement.

"Who would like to share his story this morning?" the teacher asked.

Four students raised their hands. Mbaya and Stadi were among the four students. Many students pointed at Mbaya since they hadn't heard him speak in class.

"Mbaya, share your story with the rest of the class, will you?" the teacher asked.

Mbaya stood up and went to the front of the class. He looked down in deep thought and then faced the class.

"The story I'm sharing with you was narrated to me by my grandmother. Once upon a time, a man and his son owned a donkey. Because they were very poor, they decided to take the donkey to the market, sell it, and get money to buy food. They tied a rope around the donkey's neck. As they trudged along the road, the son led the donkey by pulling the rope. His father went behind the donkey to nudge it move forward using his walking stick. One mile away from their home, they encountered a crowd of men and women," Mbaya narrated.

"Where are you taking the donkey?" an aged man from the crowd asked.

"We're taking it to the market for sale," the son's father replied.

"You son should be ashamed of yourself! Your father should be riding on the donkey while you lead it to the market. Your father will be very tired by the time he gets to the market," the aged man said.

"Father and son stopped beside the road. Father mounted the donkey's back and his son continued to lead the donkey to the market," Mbaya said.

"Father, son, and the donkey had traveled for half a mile when they found a group of young men playing by the road side," Mbaya narrated.

"Your son looks very tired. Why don't you allow him to ride on the donkey to recover his strength? The young men asked the father.

"Son it's your turn. Ride on the donkey," the father told his son.

"With the son riding on the donkey and the father leading it on, the donkey's legs gave way and fell in the middle of the road.

This incident attracted many passers-by," said Mbaya.

"Help! Help!" Father and son shouted.

"Father, son, and the passers-by lifted the donkey to its feet. The donkey was given water and straw. Meanwhile, father and son were advised to carry the donkey on their shoulders to ensure it looked healthy on arrival at the market. Immediately, father and son fetched ropes and a strong long wooden pole. They tied the donkey's legs at the middle of the wooden pole, lifted and carried it on their shoulders as they went to the market," Mbaya narrated.

"Interesting but how did it end, Mbaya? The teacher asked.

"Father and son carried the donkey over a shaky river bridge near the market. As they looked at their own shadows in the water below them, the donkey loosened its legs from the pole, fell at the edge of the bridge and tumbled into the river with a huge splash," Mbaya said.

"That is a great story. Congratulations!" the teacher told Mbaya.

"Yes!" the whole class replied and clapped for Mbaya.

"Thank you very much," Mbaya replied smiling broadly.

"What lesson do you learn from Mbaya's story?" the teacher asked.

"The story teaches us that we should stick to decisions we make and carefully evaluate other peoples' suggestions before putting them into practice," Mbaya replied.

"Very good," the teacher told Mbaya.

"Who's next to share a story? Raise up your hand," the teacher asked.

The students raised up their hands except Mbaya.

"Ok, Stadi you are next," the teacher said.

Stadi stood up beside his desk and started talking.

"I was about six years old when my grandfather told me the story am about to narrate to you. Many seasons ago, two boys refused to obey their parents. They never did any domestic chores given to them. Accompanied by two dogs, they went out to hunt for antelopes, rabbits and birds for food. They chased antelopes across savannas, forests, valleys and rivers. They were vagabonds. During this time, children aged five to six years disappeared from the boys' village and were never found. One day, as the two boys chased an antelope across the forest, they saw smoke emanating from the thickest part of the forest," Stadi told the class.

"Who could live in that part of the forest? The boys wondered. "Let's find out," one boy said.

"They held their dogs tightly and gingerly approached the source of the smoke. As they watched the smoke, a tall fat man come out toward them and the dogs barked ceaselessly. He held a huge machete but smiled at them," Stadi narrated.

"Hey boys, come up here. The tall fat man led the boys inside a cave. He offered them some roasted bananas and water for food. After eating and drinking, the tall fat man asked the boys to look after his abode while he went to fetch more food for them," Stadi narrated.

"Come and see. Look through this hole in the wall. What do you see? One boy asked the other.

"Skeletons and more skeletons," the second boy replied.

"The two boys were so scared that they decided to run away. No sooner had they gone out of the cave than the tall fat man arrived. They ran in different directions. As the tall fat man chased one of the boys, one dog jumped on him. He slashed it with his machete and continued to chase the boy. He caught up with the boy, dragged him back to the cave and strangled him to death,"

Stadi told the class.

"Poor boy, what a terrible end! What happened to the second boy?" the teacher asked.

"The second boy ran as fast as he could and reported the incident to the nearest police station. At 6.00 p.m. that day, police went to the cave and condoned the area. The tall fat man was asked to come out of the cave with his hands raised up. He did. He was handcuffed and he confessed that he was a murderer and had killed a boy and his dog that day.

"Wow! What a thrilling and scary story! The end of the story was good since the murderer was caught. Congratulations Stadi!" the teacher said.

"What did you learn from the story?" the teacher asked the class.

"We must obey our parents," one student replied.

"Curiosity is good but one must be cautiously curious. The two boys in the story were eager to find out where the smoke came from. One of them was killed while the other one helped in the arrest of the murderer," a second student replied.

"That is an excellent observation," the teacher commented. "Our time is up and we'll continue tomorrow. Have a good day," the teacher said.

As the students went out to a math class, they looked happy and excited by the stories Mbaya and Stadi shared in class.

"You remember you did a math test last Friday? I'm glad to inform you that you did well. Out of the 20 sums, no one got less 18 sums correct. You will collect your graded papers at the end of the class and make corrections of any sums done incorrectly," the teacher said.

"Will you want to see the corrections, sir?" Stadi asked.

"Yes, when you come to class tomorrow," the teacher replied. "For today, open up the last chapter of your math textbook. You will learn how to add, subtract, and multiply numbers that have three digits. For example, 364+372+385, 364-278, and 362 multiply by 173. You will also learn how division is done with similar numbers, such as 390 divide by say 15," the teacher explained as he demonstrated how to tackle each sum on the chalkboard. "Any questions?" the teacher asked.

Many hands shot up to ask questions.

"Yes sir. How do I remember to carry a number in my mind to add it to the next number during addition?" Stadi asked.

"Well, write it down somewhere you can see it on your paper. Don't forget to add it to the next number in your addition. Okay? The teacher explained.

"I didn't understand what you did to be able to subtract a large number from a small one," another student asked the teacher.

"That's a good question. Take our example of 364 minus 278. Write down 364 and below it write 278 such that two is below three and seven below six and eight below four. Start subtracting from the right. You will not be able to subtract eight from four because four is smaller than eight. You will borrow one from six of the top numbers, and add it to four to get 14. Subtract eight from 14 to get six. Since you borrowed one from six in the top numbers, you were left with five as a middle number. Again, five is smaller than seven in lower numbers. Borrow one from three, the first digit of the top numbers, and add it to the five to get fifteen. Subtract seven, the middle digit of the bottom numbers to get eight. So, the answer is 86. Is it clear now?" the teacher asked.

"Yes sir," the students said.

"Remember when to carry numbers in your head during

addition and multiplication and when to borrow numbers during subtraction. For class practice, do the exercise in your math textbook and the next exercise for your homework," the teacher instructed.

As the teacher moved from student to student helping them in their math difficulties, the bell rang for tea and coffee break and the students went out.

"What will you have, coffee or tea?" Stadi asked Mbaya.

"Tea please," Mbaya replied.

"I didn't really understand the teacher's explanation regarding the borrowing and the carrying of numbers in one's head when subtracting and multiplying. Did you, Mbaya? Stadi asked.

"I think I did. Nonetheless, let's confirm as we do the homework this evening after supper," replied Mbaya.

"Okay, agreed," Stadi replied.

Tea and coffee break was over and the bell was rung to resume school activities.

"Oh, let's hurry for our English reading class," Stadi said looking at the wall clock.

"Take out your English reading text book," the teacher said. "As you know this is your last term in grade two. From now, you will be graded on reading and an aggregate grade given to you at the end of the term in December," the teacher informed the class. "Any questions?" the teacher asked.

"No madam," the class unanimously replied.

"Well then, open your reading text on the story about the Sun and the Wind. Each person will read two sentences until all have read. We'll start with Stadi and move rightwards," the teacher instructed.

Stadi read his sentences quickly and pronounced the

words clearly. Many other students read their sentences but mispronounced some words.

"It's your turn to read," the teacher pointed at Mbaya.

Mbaya stood up, cleared his throat and read slowly, audibly, and fluently.

"Wow! Wow! That was very good reading!" the teacher exclaimed.

The class, including the teacher, clapped for Mbaya and congratulated him for reading his sentences so well.

It was time for lunch when the English reading class ended.

"Mbaya and Stadi, would you remain behind for a few minutes?" the teacher asked.

"Yes, madam," Mbaya and Stadi replied.

"I'm grateful to both of you for working as a team. Mbaya is now able to read without stuttering and sweating like before. Did the story book I gave you help?" the teacher asked Mbaya.

"Yes, together with the help from Stadi and others," said Mbaya.

"This is a gift for you Mbaya and for you Stadi," the teacher said as she presented each one of them with a new story book.

"Thank you very much, madam," Mbaya and Stadi replied.

"Today is my happiest day in school. I can't believe I read my sentences so well. Many thanks, Stadi, for not giving up on me and for your persistence," Mbaya said as they were eating lunch.

"Thank you Mbaya. You read better than I. I'm very happy for you. Let's go for our siesta before the outdoor activities at 2.00 p.m.," Stadi said.

At 2.00 p.m., all the students, including their teachers went to the playing field for athletics competition. There were three dormitories at CRC and each selected its best athletes to run 100 yards, 200 yards, long jump, and high jump.

"We'll start this afternoon's athletics by running 100 yards. I want the first three students, one from each dormitory to come forward and lined up at the starting point. On your marks! Get seeet! Go!" the athletics teacher shouted.

"Faster! Faster! Hurry hurry uuup!" students and teachers cheered their runners.

"Number one is dormitory two, number two is dormitory one, and number three is dormitory three," the announcer said.

"What happened to you, Stadi? You are number three?" the teacher and dormitory three students asked.

"I had a crump on my leg," replied Stadi.

The athletics teacher called up the second group of 100 yard runners.

"On your marks! Get seeet! Go!" The teacher shouted.

"Hurry on! Faster! Faster! Faaster! The crowd cheered.

"Number one is dormitory one, number two is dormitory two, and number three is dormitory three," the announcer said.

"Congratulations Mbaya," the teacher and students of dormitory one congratulated Mbaya.

"The next activity is long jump. Let's all move to the long jump area. I want the three long jump candidates to line up according to their dormitories," the athletics teacher instructed.

"Dormitory number one candidate, come on. One, two, three, jump!" the teacher shouted.

"In long jump, dormitory one is number one, dormitory three is number is number two, and dormitory two is number three," the announcer said.

"Congratulations Mbaya for your sterling performance in long jump!" dormitory one students exclaimed.

Athletics competition got heated. Each dormitory head gathered their students to map out winning strategies for the remaining two athletics activities, running of 200 yards and the high jump.

"Candidates for 200 yards, come on here!" the athletics teacher ordered. "On your marks! Get seeet! Go!" he shouted.

One student from dormitory two had started running before the athletics teacher said "go" and the spectators booed.

"Come back! Come back!" the athletics teacher shouted. "Get onto your lanes. If you start running before the word "go" you will be disqualified from this race. Do you understand?" the athletics teacher asked.

"Yes, sir," the students replied.

"On your marks! Get seeet! Go!" the athletics teacher shouted.

"Hurry up! Faster! Faster and don't look back!" spectators shouted to the runners.

The student from dormitory two was ahead in the race most of the time, but about ten feet from the finish line, he staggered and fell to the ground. The student from dormitory one ran past and won the race. Meanwhile, the student who fell to the ground was taken to a nearby clinic for treatment.

"Well done Mbaya! You've done us proud," students of dormitory one students said.

"Here are the results of 200 yards race and the high jump. Remember that both events went on simultaneously. Dormitory one won the 200 yards race and was number two in high jump. Dormitory three was second in 200 yards race and number two in high jump. Dormitory two was number three in both 200 yards race and the high jump. Overall, dormitory one is the champion of the year, dormitory three is number two, and dormitory two is number three. Well done everybody," the announcer said.

It was 5.00 p.m. The students vacated the athletics field and went to their dormitories to shower and refresh themselves.

"What a great afternoon we had today! I've enjoyed participating in the sports and to watch others participate, especially you, Stadi," Mbaya commented.

"Thank you. I was thrilled to watch you win 100 and 200 yards races. You are truly talented as an athlete," Stadi replied.

After supper Stadi and Mbaya went to do their math and English homework. They felt enthused as they finished the homework and retired to their respective dormitories for the night.

Mbaya's final days at CRC

After breakfast, Mbaya went to see the counselor as usual. He knocked at the counselor's office door.

"Come on in!" the counselor said. "Welcome and have a seat. Would you like a cup of tea or coffee with some biscuits?" the counselor asked.

"No sir, since I've just had breakfast," replied Mbaya.

"I'm very happy to hear of your great progress since you came to CRC. You have excelled in athletics and recently in math and reading. You also work very well with your classmates and teachers. You are also resourceful, friendly, and healthy. In other words, you have become a better person since you came to CRC," the counselor informed Mbaya.

"I'm thankful to you for many things, especially for arranging the visit I made to the Pastor's home. I'm also grateful to my teachers, the students, and the CRC community who have contributed a lot to help me reform," replied Mbaya.

"You are welcome," the counselor said. "Last week, we received a letter from the chief of your home area requesting to know how you are doing since you came here. Apparently, your parents want to know whether your behavior has changed for better and if so, when you would be released to join them," the counselor informed Mbaya.

Mbaya was dumbfounded to hear that his family, especially his father, was eager to receive him back home.

"CRC has become my home. I love it. How shall I be received by family and the community at home after the havoc I caused?" Mbaya wondered.

"You look worried at the prospects of joining your family and the community?" the counselor asked Mbaya.

"Yes sir, I'm concerned how Kogi, the boy I brutally hurt when coming from school will react toward me. How will my father treat me? He swooned after he knew I lied to him that I went to school when I didn't," replied Mbaya.

"I see, I understand, but your behavior has changed for the better since you've been here in the last three months. Also, remember that actions speak louder than words. You will need to apologize to Kogi, your dad, and any others you hurt before you came to CRC. Will you do that?" the counselor asked.

"Yes, sir," Mbaya replied.

"Great, see you again later," the counselor told Mbaya.

Mbaya moved on to his math class.

"Good morning class? I want to inform you that this is your last math class in grade two. We've come to the end of term. Stadi will collect your homework and leave it on my desk for grading. Most of you will be sent back to your homes to join grade three in schools there. Any questions?" the math teacher asked.

"Yes, what about our grades?" one student asked.

"That's a good question. The counselor will inform you of everything including your grades. Nonetheless, all of you did well in math," the teacher replied.

"Thank you sir, we enjoyed your personal concern of each one of us and your good teaching in math," Stadi said on behalf of the class.

"Clap! Clap! Clap! Clap! Clap!" the whole class clapped.

"Oh, thank you all. Thank you and best of luck for your future," the teacher said.

The bell for the next class was rung and the students rushed to the class.

"Hello class? As this is your last class with me in grade two, I want to see how well you spell words. Open a new page in your exercise book. Listen and write down the sentence I will read to you. Okay?" the teacher asked.

"Yes madam," the students replied looking at the teacher attentively.

"The quick brown fox jumped over the lazy dogs," the teacher read the sentence very slowly three times. "In your spare time, examine this sentence and you will find that all the alphabets, A to Z, are represented in it. Leave your exercise books on my desk for grading. Thank you and goodbye," the teacher said.

As students moved out of the English class, Mbaya and Stadi were left behind.

"On behalf of Stadi and myself, I wish to express my thanks to you for helping me so much. You appointed Stadi to help me in English and he has been wonderful as a friend. You gave me two story books that have helped me read a great deal. Thank you so much madam," Mbaya said.

"Most welcome. Both of you have been great students in my class," the teacher told them as they parted.

It was time for tea and coffee break.

"You know what Stadi? I was informed by the counselor that I will be going home next week. I will miss your company very much. Let's exchange our home addresses to help us keep in touch through letter writing," Mbaya suggested.

"That's an excellent idea," replied Stadi. "Here is my home address."

"And here is mine," Mbaya said.

"Although I haven't been informed, I know I'll be going home also. They evaluate you on three things to be sent back home; your behavior since arrival at CRC, your academic performance, and your relationship with other people. I have been good at all of them. Two of our classmates may not be allowed to go home because of their behavior," Stadi said.

"What will happen to the two classmates after we go? Mbaya asked.

"They will be at CRC for another three months after which, if they don't behave well, they will be sent to another severer rehab for a whole year," said Stadi.

"Thank goodness we're out of that situation," Mbaya said.

"Oh yes, things could have been worse!" Stadi commented.

The last week at CRC

Mbaya reported at the counselor's office the following Monday at 8.10 a.m. He knocked at the counselor's office door three times but there was no answer. As he waited outside the counselor's office, he looked to his right and saw the counselor chatting with two CRC officials outside the office of the president.

"Hey Mbaya, don't go I'm coming!" shouted the counselor.

"How are you? I'm sorry I'm late today because we had a staff meeting led by the CRC president. The CRC president is meeting everybody in the hall at 9.00 a.m. today since this is the last week of this term. The meeting will end at 10.00 a.m. Please, be here at the office 10.20 a.m. for further information," the counselor told Mbaya.

"Okay sir," Mbaya said as he stood up to go to the hall for the meeting.

At 9.00 a.m., the students, the teachers, the counselors, and other rehab workers were seated in the hall. It was so quiet that one could hear a pin drop. As soon as the CRC president and his deputy appeared, everybody stood up.

"Thank you and take your seats. As you know, we have come to the end of this term. You and I are eager to hear words of wisdom from CRC president. Mr. President, speak to the people," the deputy president said.

"Thank you very much for those kind words, Mr. Deputy President. I wish to thank the teachers, the counselors, and the workers for their hard work in ensuring there were no nasty incidents in this rehab. Indeed, we have rehabilitated more students this term than any other time before. Congratulations! Many thanks go to my deputy who did a lot of work when I was away on vacation and in conferences. I want to thank our students, many of whom have behaved fabulously, considering the condition for which they were brought here. Many of them will be released back to their parents and communities this week. I believe that we have taught them, not only academics, but life principles that will continue to guide them in life. A few of you, students, will remain here for another term for further help, and, if you do not change your behavior, other steps will be taken. Your counselors will give you full details today after this meeting. Thank you and best of luck to all," the president concluded his speech.

Many students came out of the meeting wondering whether they were going home or remaining at CRC for another term. Not so for Mbaya.

It was 10.20 a.m.

"How do you feel after the president's speech?" the counselor asked Mbaya. "At least you knew you would be going home from our discussion last week," the counselor added.

"On one hand I feel good and on the other hand, I feel uneasy because my new behavior may make others at home unwelcoming to me," replied Mbaya.

"Well, that isn't unusual. Reentry into one's environment after training presents some challenges but we'll try to minimize them for you. You will also have to do the best you know how," the counselor admonished.

"Thank you, sir. How will you minimize my reentry challenges?" Mbaya asked.

"First we have sent a letter to your chief informing him of your good character, your excellence in math, sports, and reading. We asked the chief to contact your parents to meet you at his office on Friday at 2.00 p.m. You will be accompanied by the Pastor and driven to the chief's office by a CRC driver. On arrival, the Pastor will explain to the chief, your parents, and community leaders that you have changed for the better. He will answer any questions about you on behalf of CRC and you will answer any questions directed to you by those present. Be prepared," the counselor explained.

"That sounds good and interesting," Mbaya said.

"Good. Remember you've two days to prepare yourself and say good bye to your comrades before going home," the counselor said.

"Thank you sir for your help," Mbaya said as he stood up to go.

"Welcome. See you here on Friday at 8.10 a.m.," the counselor said.

That evening after supper, Mbaya and Stadi met with their classmates in the common room. They laughed, hugged, and embraced to bid one another goodbye but two of their classmates looked unhappy. They were not going home.

"Please, remember me in your prayers," one of the unhappy students requested.

"And me too," the second student also requested.

"We will," Mbaya and Stadi replied.

The following day, Mbaya woke up as usual at 6.00 a.m. There were no classes. The sun had risen and the sky was brilliantly blue. The grass in the compound was lush and green as water fell on it like rain drops from the sprinklers. The gardener, who worked in the compound, was busy assembling water sprinklers to water various parts of the compound.

"What shall I do before breakfast? Mbaya wondered. "Well, I'll clean my shirts, pants, socks, brush my shoes, collect my books, and pack all of them in my box ready for the journey home tomorrow," Mbaya thought to himself.

At 6.45 a.m., Mbaya had washed his clothes, collected his books, and brushed his shoes. He was arranging them in his box when the breakfast bell rang. He ran to the dining hall to have his breakfast of porridge made out of corn flour. As he came out, he had a voice calling his name from the parking lot.

"Hello Mbaya! Helloooo!" a familiar voice called out.

Mbaya stopped and listened carefully. He dashed out toward the caller.

"Hello Caleb! What a pleasant surprise for me early this morning!" Mbaya exclaimed.

Mbaya and Caleb hugged each other warmly.

"How is the Pastor and the rest of your family?" Mbaya inquired.

"They are very well, thank you. You see, word came to us that you are leaving for home tomorrow morning. Is it true?" Caleb asked.

"Yes, you're correct," replied Mbaya.

"I wanted you to visit us a second time before you leave CRC, but it doesn't look it will happen. Well, my mother was coming to town for shopping this morning and she dropped me here to bid you goodbye," Caleb told Mbaya.

"That is very kind of you, Caleb. I will never forget your help and kindness when I visited your home. Thank you so, so much," Mbaya said tearfully as he embraced Caleb.

"You are most welcome,' Caleb said. "My father told me that

he and the CRC driver will drive you home. Correct?" asked Caleb.

"Yes, according to the CRC counselor," Mbaya replied.

"Do you mind if I accompany you along with my father and the CRC driver?" Caleb requested.

"Not at all, you are most welcome," Mbaya replied as he smiled broadly.

"Many thanks," Caleb said. "Hey look over there at the parking lot. That's mother waiting for me. Come and say hi to her," Caleb requested.

Caleb's mother was parking the van after her morning shopping when both Caleb and Mbaya approached her.

"How are you, Mbaya?" Caleb's mother asked.

"I'm very well, madam," Mbaya replied. "You are very kind to bring Caleb here on my last day," Mbaya added.

"Thanks. We have all missed you since you visited us," Caleb's mother told Mbaya.

"And I too have missed you all. You've been like family since I came to CRC," Mbaya said.

"By the way, have you heard from your parents since you came to CRC?" Caleb's mother asked Mbaya.

"Not directly, but I was informed by the counselor that my parents want to know about my behavior since I came to CRC," Mbaya replied.

"In my family, we know you as a well behaved young man. We love you. We pray that you will be able to reconnect well with your parents and siblings," Caleb's mother told Mbaya.

"Thanks for those kind words about me. I was also informed

by the CRC counselor that a good report about me was sent to the chief of our area," Mbaya informed Caleb's mother.

"That's great. By the way, please, accept this gift and enjoy with your friends what is contained in it," Caleb's mother said.

"Many thanks for your kindness, madam," Mbaya said.

"See you tomorrow as agreed," Caleb waved Mbaya as his mother drove off.

"Bye-bye," Mbaya said and waved them back smiling.

Mbaya rushed to the common room carrying his gift in the plastic bag without knowing what it was. He opened the plastic bag.

"Wow, wow, chunks of grilled beef, donuts, and four bottles of coca cola. I haven't had anything like this for a long time. What about Stadi, my friend? I'll look for him to enjoy the feast together," Mbaya gladly thought.

Mbaya hid his gift in one of the cupboards in the common room. He went out toward the next dormitory looking for his friend, Stadi.

"How are you doing this morning?" Mbaya asked Stadi.

"Fine, but I've been very busy cleaning my clothes, sorting out my books, and arranging them in my box ready to go home tomorrow," Stadi replied.

"Well, I did the same this morning but didn't put them in my box. I hope to do it this evening after supper. By the way, would you mind accompanying me to the common room? Mbaya asked.

"Let's go. After all this is our last day together here at CRC," replied Stadi.

On their way to the common room, Mbaya and Stadi saw

two of their classmates seated outside their dormitory.

"Hi! Do you mind joining us in the common room?" Mbaya asked.

"No! We'll join you, thanks" one classmate replied to Mbaya.

The common room was clean with a capacity to hold 20 people when seated. The floor was concrete with grey terrazzo coating for ease of cleaning. Fixed on the wall about six feet from the floor was a box that had a radio. Students listened to local and world news and contemporary folk music from the radio during their leisure time.

"Hey Stadi, switch on the radio for music. Let's enjoy our last evening together," Mbaya said.

As music was playing, Mbaya opened the drawer containing the gift from Caleb's mother- four large pieces of grilled beef, donuts, and four bottles of coca cola in the brown paper bag. He laid them on the table.

"Wow! This is great! What a feast we'll have!" Stadi exclaimed.

"What a generous person you are, Mbaya to invite us to this feast! I haven't had grilled beef and a coca cola drink for a long time," said one of Mbaya's classmates.

"And me too! Thank you very much for inviting us," said the other of Mbaya's classmates.

"You are all welcome to enjoy the feast," Mbaya said. "In case you are wondering how I got these items of food and drinks, let me explain. You all know the Pastor associated with CRC. His wife, the mother to my friend Caleb, bought them for me to enjoy with my friends, and, you are my friends," Mbaya explained.

"Many, many thanks. You are truly a friend indeed," the three classmates of Mbaya said in unison.

"You too are sincerely my friends. Stadi, you've been a special person to me. You've struggled with me as I tried to catch up with math and reading and we succeeded. Many thanks to you," Mbaya told his friends.

"It was my pleasure to work with you. You are a very resourceful person. See what you've done for us, this feast," Stadi replied.

As Mbaya and his friends were feasting in the common room, the lunch bell rang.

"Should we go for lunch in the dining hall or continue with our feast?" Mbaya asked his comrades.

"Oh yes, we must go for lunch and eat a little food or not eat at all. Since this is the last day of term, a roll call will be taken of students from each dormitory," Stadi advised.

Mbaya and his comrades hurriedly cleaned the table, the floor around the table, and threw away the garbage they had amassed during their feast. They ran to the dining commons for lunch.

"Good afternoon everybody!" the counselor shouted before lunch was served to the students.

"Good afternoon sir!" the students shouted back.

"At the end of each term, it is our tradition to recognize three students who made remarkable positive change at CRC. We evaluate their behavioral change, academics, and interpersonal relationships. As an encouragement for more improvement when they leave here, CRC offers to pay one year's tuition for grade three in the school of their choice. It can be a day school or a boarding school. Okay so far?" the counselor asked.

"Yes! Yes!" students said in unison.

"When you hear your name called out, please, stand up

to be seen by everybody here. Those who fulfilled the criteria mentioned above are: Stadi Tosha from dormitory three, Mbaya Zungu from dormitory one, and Jia Defu from dormitory two. Please, clap for them," the counselor requested.

"Clap, clap, clap, clap…" everybody clapped.

"Thanks. You may go on with your lunch," the counselor concluded.

There was a great excitement in the dining hall as students ate their lunch. Stadi, Mbaya, and Jia were overjoyed and could hardly speak or eat lunch.

After lunch, Mbaya and Stadi went out together. They hugged each other with excitement, bade each other goodbye and headed to their respective dormitories.

"Who will help me to choose a good boarding school for my grade three class next year? My father, though a primary school teacher, will order me to go to a school I don't like. Oh yes, Caleb's father, the Pastor, will be of great help to me," Mbaya thought as he packed his few belongings in his box.

As Mbaya was coming out of the dining hall after supper, the counselor waved his hand and Mbaya went to see him.

"How do you feel now that you will be going home tomorrow morning? The counselor asked.

"I feel good about all the things CRC has done for me. I'm a better person than I came. But, I'm sorry to part with my classmates and to leave this environment that has been so helpful and encouraging to me. I also don't know which school I shall attend next year," Mbaya told the counselor.

"You've explained it very well. For your school next year, this is a list of schools near your home and other places. Select the school that you like or ask your parents to help you select one when you get home. By the way, these are copies of your CRC reports for you to keep. I wish you a safe journey home and warm relations with your family and the community in your area," the counselor admonished Mbaya.

That night, Mbaya went to bed earlier than usual. While in bed, his mind got clouded with his impending unclear future at his parent's home.

"What shall I tell Kogi whom I hurt so badly and for no reason except to boost my ego? Will the community we terrorized and stole things from accept me back? How will my father treat me after letting him down so much? What shall I say to the people at the chief's office when we arrive there? Oh my... what shall I do?" Mbaya turned from right to left in his bed many times as he thought about these questions.

The following day at breakfast, Mbaya looked haggard, gloomy, and exhausted like someone who had been working throughout the night.

"Hey, are you ill?" Stadi asked Mbaya, his friend.

"No, I'm physically fit but my mind isn't. I didn't sleep well," Mbaya replied.

"Why?" Stadi asked.

"Being at CRC has been very liberating. I dread what will happen when I get home," replied Mbaya.

"Oh yes, I agree with you. But, remember that you, I, and others were brought here for rehabilitation because we were bad boys. Your behavior and mine have greatly improved. We are better than when we came to CRC. That's why we have been released back to our parents. Besides, we have great recommendations, free tuition for the next class and CRC staff to take us home. This should cheer you up. Don't you think so?" Stadi asked.

Mbaya Leaves CRC

"I guess you are correct. I'm tending to look on the bad side of things rather on the good side. But all the same, at 2.00 p.m. today when we get at the chief's office, I will be forced to answer various questions from my father, the chief, Kogi's father and perhaps other village elders who will be present. I have no idea what they will ask and how I'll answer them," Mbaya said.

"Thank you for calling out my name. I was engrossed in watching the various models of vehicles parked out here," Mbaya told the CRC driver. "Look over there! That is the Pastor and Caleb," Mbaya told the CRC driver.

"I have no clue either. Nonetheless, I think whatever you're asked, show confidence, courage, and courtesy," Stadi suggested.

"Oh yes, I see them. Let's get near them," the CRC driver said.

"Good morning Pastor" the CRC deriver said.

"Many thanks. That's great advice to me," Mbaya replied.

"Good morning," the Pastor replied.

"Best of luck," Stadi said.

The CRC driver and Mbaya came out of the minibus to join the Pastor and his "Mbaya" at the parking lot. It was a sunny morning and most of the sky was blue with few clouds scattered over it. A cool breeze blew over the parking lot making people feel good and comfortable. The parking lot was a beehive of activities as students and their guardians moved hither and thither, some talking.

Mbaya and Stadi hugged and bade each other their final goodbyes. They ran to their respective dormitories, picked up their luggage ready to go home.

"Hi Mbaya, come on the journey" the Pastor called out.

They joined hands and the Pastor prayed. "We thank God for his grace and mercy for each one of us. We thank him also that Mbaya has been given permission by CRC authorities to go home and join his family after one term. Oh God, protect us on the journey. Give us a good time as we meet with the chief, Mbaya's father, community elders and other officials. Give Mbaya wisdom he needs to join his family and the rest of the community. I pray this in the name of Jesus. And all said, Amen."

The journey to Mbaya's home started at 8.00 a.m. Unlike the

van that brought Mbaya to CRC three months ago, the CRC van was newer and faster.

"How are you feeling now that you are going home?" The Pastor asked Mbaya.

"I'm very jittery," replied Mbaya.

"I understand your situation. But, what particularly gives you jitters?" the Pastor asked.

"I'm afraid of my father's reaction toward me. You see he swooned when he knew I was involved in theft before I came to CRC. He was sent to the hospital in a police car. I also fear Kogi, my former classmate, whom I injured on our way home from school," Mbaya replied.

"You are correct. These are real issues. However, you've reformed after your stint at CRC. Haven't you?" the Pastor said.

"Yes, Pastor. But how shall I convince them about it?" Mbaya asked.

"Actions speak louder than words. Your consistent good behavior will eventually convince them. You will also need to ask them to forgive you for the hurt you caused them before going to CRC," the Pastor advised.

"Dad, please tell the chief, Mbaya's father, and others present how well behaved and creative Mbaya was when he stayed with us on the weekend," Caleb asked his father, the Pastor.

"Okay, Caleb. I'll also explain Mbaya's CRC report to the chief, Mbaya's father, and other elders present at the chief's office. Then there will be a time for questions and answers concerning Mbaya," the Pastor said.

"The CRC counselor told me that I might be asked questions at the chief's office. Is it true?" Mbaya asked.

"Yes it's true. Make sure you listen to each question and take time to think before you answer," the Pastor replied.

"Do you know which school you will attend next year?" Caleb asked Mbaya.

"Not yet. I have a list of schools given to me by CRC counselor," Mbaya replied.

"It's time we had some lunch before we proceed to the chief's office," the Pastor announced.

"Yes," replied Caleb and Mbaya in a chorus.

The driver veered slowly to the right and drove to a gas station. A few yards away, was a restaurant with a billboard written on it "Traveler's Restaurant." The driver refueled the minibus with gasoline while the Pastor, Caleb, and Mbaya went to the restrooms. Finally, the four people sat around a table at one corner of the restaurant.

"Good afternoon? How may I help you?" the waiter asked.

"We want to have lunch and drinks," the Pastor replied.

"Here is the menu," the waiter said.

"Thanks you. Give us a minute to study it," the Pastor replied.

"What do you want to eat and drink?" the Pastor asked his companions.

"French fries (chips), chicken and a medium coca cola drink," said the CRC driver.

"And you?" the Pastor asked Caleb and Mbaya.

"The same food and drink as the driver," Caleb and Mbaya replied.

The Pastor waved the waiter to take the orders.

"Bring three plates of chicken and French fries and three medium coca cola drinks, and, one fish and French fries and a cup of hot tea," the Pastor said.

As they were having lunch, Mbaya produced the list of schools given to him by the CRC counselor. He gave it to the Pastor.

"Please, advise me which boarding school to attend next year. As perhaps you know, CRC will pay tuition for me the whole year," Mbaya said.

"That's great, Mbaya. Perhaps Caleb might also help," the Pastor commented.

"I would recommend my school to Mbaya. It's a boarding school with grades one to eight. Next to our primary school, is an excellent boarding high school. Every year, this high school gives scholarships to five best students from our primary school. The best students are those who attain two As and a B, in math, English, and science in the final grade eight examination, have good character, and good interpersonal relations," Caleb advised.

"Mbaya, what do you think of Caleb's suggestion?" asked the Pastor.

"It's truly a great suggestion. I like it," Mbaya replied.

Meanwhile, the waiter handed the food bill to the Pastor.

"Hey waiter!" the Pastor called.

"Is the bill wrong?" the waiter asked.

"Yes, we were served three medium coca cola drinks and one cup of tea. Not four sodas. Okay?" the Pastor replied.

"Oh, oh, I'm sorry. Let me get you another bill," the waiter said.

The Pastor paid the corrected food bill and put the receipt in his wallet. Outside the restaurant, the sun shone. The skies were cloudless. It was hot but not muggy.

"How far are we from our destination?" the Pastor asked the driver.

"About an hour's drive," the driver replied.

After ten minutes of driving from the restaurant, the driver left the paved main road and followed a side road that was not paved. It was a gravel road. The gravel made the road so bumpy that the passengers held to their seats as they were being thrown up and down from the seats. Furthermore, they were traveling uphill. But, the country side was spectacular to behold. There were hills covered with green vegetation, rivers and rivulets flowed down the hillsides. In the valleys along the river banks, were dwelling houses from which smoke billowed. Cattle, goats, and sheep were grazing along the river banks and on the hill sides where grass was lush. Taking care of these domestic animals were elderly men and young boys. They stood two by two at strategic points on the hills and the valleys to ensure that no cattle, goats or sheep strayed into nearby fields of corn and beans.

"Wow, this is fantastic scenery!" Caleb commented.

"It is. When we go over this hill, you will see a different a kind of scenery," the driver said.

"Mbaya, have you been here before?" Caleb asked.

"Yes, when I was coming to CRC. I was asleep for the most of the journey. I was also scared because I didn't know where they were taking me," Mbaya replied.

"Well, what a blessed day we have! The sky is brilliantly blue, the sun is shining and yet it is cool and not humid. This is great weather," the Pastor commented.

"Yes dad, but look westwards. The sky seems to touch the ground. What a beauty!" Caleb said.

"That's a range of mountains where the sky seems to touch the ground," the driver said.

"One day, I would like to climb that range of mountains to see what lies beyond it," said Caleb.

"That's good ambition. You could do it when you go to high

school or college. They have programs for mountain climbing," the Pastor told Caleb.

"It must very expensive to pay for it?" asked Caleb.

"Yes, it is expensive in a number of ways. First, one must train for mountain climbing by doing strenuous exercises for months. Secondly, one must buy mountain climbing gear that is required. Thirdly, one must be able pay for various other expenses, such as, medical, residential, and insurance," the Pastor informed Caleb.

"It sounds very challenging," Caleb said.

"Sure, it is. It helps to build character in terms of perseverance, fosters ability to work in teams, and to obey instructions," the Pastor told Caleb.

"That sounds great. One day Mbaya and I hope to climb that range of mountains. Do you agree, Mbaya?" Caleb asked.

"Definitely, I would love it," Mbaya said.

As the Pastor, Caleb, and Mbaya were engaged in an animated conversation about mountain climbing, the driver was driving uphill and trying to negotiate a blind corner. Suddenly, everybody was thrown forwards from the seats in the minibus. There was loud screeching noise as the driver applied emergency breaks.

"Oh, oh, what has gone wrong?" the Pastor asked.

"Look over there in the bushes. That antelope dashed across the road as it was being pursued by a dog. I applied emergency breaks to avoid collision," the driver explained.

"That was scary," Mbaya said.

"My legs are still shaking. But, I'm glad we are still alive," Caleb said.

"Let's come out of the minibus, stretch ourselves and breathe some fresh air," the Pastor said.

"How much longer is the journey to the chief's office?" Caleb asked the driver.

"After we negotiate this bend, it will take us about twenty-five minutes to get there," the driver replied.

"There is a big open air market near the chief's office and today is a market day," Mbaya said.

"Look over there! Is that the open air market you talked about, Mbaya?" Caleb asked.

"Yes, it is," Mbaya replied.

As the driver approached the open air market, we saw many stone buildings. A few buildings had two storeys but most had a single storey. These buildings were shops and restaurants built around the open air market. They formed a rectangle between which the open air market was located. Road inlets into the market were from east, west, north and south. Similarly, there were exits out of the market from the same directions. On the western side of the market was a bus terminus where public vehicles unloaded their passengers. Near the bus terminus was a gas station.

"Let's move on to the gas station. I need to refuel the minibus," the driver said.

The gas station had four gas pumping stations all of which were occupied. The driver moved on and stationed the minibus near the gas station mini-shop.

"Move up here!" a gas station attendant called.

"Thanks," the driver said.

"Open up the fuel tank. I have to pump the gas manually because there is no electric power on this pump," the gas attendant said.

When the driver of the minibus was moving out of the gas station and heading toward the market, the Pastor shouted,

"Look at that signboard on our left. It reads that Chief"s

office is half a mile up the hill. Let's have a cup of tea in the restaurant nearest to us before going there," the Pastor said.

We entered the restaurant.

"Waiter, please serve us with four cups of tea and donuts as well," the Pastor ordered.

As we drank tea and ate donuts, we heard some men in the restaurant discussing Mbaya's case. It seemed to have polarized the community of his area.

The pastor paid for the tea and the donuts. We got in to the minibus and headed for the chief's office up the hill. The road to the chief's office was well maintained. The gravel on the road had been crushed and pressed to make it smooth all weather road. On both sides of the road was a cypress hedge that was well manicured. The cypress hedge surrounded the area where the chief's office was located. Interspersing the cypress hedge were bougainvillea flowers that were beautifully red. The metal gate to the chief's office was blue and fixed to two stone columns fifteen feet apart. Above the gate was a metal signboard on which was written "Chief's Office" and office working hours were shown. Two guards manned the gate and each had an AK-47 strapped across the left shoulder.

"Are you from Central Rehab Center?" one guard asked the driver.

"Yes we are," the driver replied.

"Will you, please, sign your names on this register," the guard instructed.

The Pastor signed the register.

"Park your vehicle in the parking lot in front of that office building ahead of you. Go into the office and a secretary will guide you further," the guard instructed.

The Pastor knocked at the office door.

"Come on in," a lady's voice said.

We entered the office.

"Are you from the Central Rehab Center (CRC)?" the lady asked.

"Yes, I'm the CRC Pastor. This is the CRC driver, my son Caleb, and Mbaya Zungu. We have brought Mbaya home after a satisfactory rehabilitation at CRC," the Pastor replied.

"Thank you. Please have a seat. Your meeting will start at 2.00 p.m. and I'll escort you to the conference room. Can I give you a cup of tea?" the lady asked.

"Yes, thank you," the Pastor replied.

As we were drinking tea, we saw people streaming out of the conference room and looking at us suspiciously.

"Please, follow me," the lady told us.

We followed. The lady led us to a large conference room. In the center of the conference room was an oval table with twenty chairs placed around it. One chair was different. It was wooden while others were plastic. It was maroon in color, soft to sit on, and was a swivel chair. It was the chief's seat. Walls to the right and to the left of the room had large glass windows that were fully open to allow cool air and light into the room. The chief sat on his swivel chair and six other people sat on the plastic chairs. The guide lady whispered to the chief after which we sat on the plastic seats.

Meeting at Chief's Office

"As you all know, this meeting was arranged to welcome back Zungu's son, Mbaya, after three months of rehabilitation at Central Rehab Center (CRC). We have a positive report from CRC about him. To discuss the report we have Mr. Kubwa, the community chairman, three community elders, Mbaya's mother, the police officer in-charge of this area, and myself. Would you mind introducing your people, Pastor?" the chief said.

"Thank you chief. This is is Mbaya Zungu, whom we've brought back home after a successful rehabilitation at CRC. Next is Caleb, my son and a great friend of Mbaya. Last but not least is the CRC driver who drove us up here and will drive us back. For those who don't know me, I'm the CRC Pastor," the Pastor said.

"Thanks, Pastor. We have read the positive report from CRC about Mbaya. Do you have any personal and practical knowledge of Mbaya's behavior? Why do you think he will integrate into the community without problems?" the chief asked.

"Mbaya is a different young man than he came to CRC. I've had weekly personal contacts with his teachers and counselor who affirm that Mbaya has changed for the better. The CRC report confirms it. Additionally, we invited him to our home one weekend. At first he was quiet and reserved. But, when he observed how free our children were talking to us, he opened up and became like a member of our family. Caleb can explain how close they've became," the Pastor explained.

Caleb explained, "My friend, Mbaya, suffered from fear, especially fear of reading in the presence of other people. This fear disappeared when we went to my room. He was so free with me that he read two small story books without problems. You see, he is one year older than I. However, I'm in grade six while he is in grade two. Mbaya is also very innovative. He milked one of our cows and got more milk from it than any other previous milkman."

"Many thanks, Caleb. What do you say about yourself?" the chief asked Mbaya.

Mbaya stood up as a symbol of respect, looked down for a few seconds and then looked directly at the chief.

"I'm truly sorry for disgracing my parents, what I did at school and in my community before I was sent to CRC. Nonetheless, I feel happy that I went to CRC to be rehabilitated. I thank the community elders who decided to help by sending me to CRC. I learned many good things, discovered my potential, and made a number of good friends. Caleb here is my best friend. I'm a better person," Mbaya said.

Mr. Kubwa, the community elders' chairman looked at Mbaya and said, "Thank you for what you've told us. But, as chairman of the elders, I would like to hear what your mother thinks concerning you. Mrs. Zungu, what do you think about your son?"

Mrs. Zungu approached his son Mbaya, who, at this juncture was standing up. With tears streaming from her eyes, she grabbed Mbaya, hugged him and cried uncontrollably. "This is my son and I love him. I have missed him a great deal. I thank you all for arranging for his rehabilitation at CRC and bringing him back a changed young man. However, his father is still unwell. Mbaya and his father don't see eye to eye. Mbaya's coming home to stay will worsen his father's health. Additionally, Mbaya's siblings and the community in our area feel that he let them down before he went to rehab. Some people in the community might harm him because of his previous misdeeds. Please, keep Mbaya away from our community until his father is well enough to discuss the issue. Thank you," Mbaya's mother pleaded.

"You've all heard the sentiments expressed by Mrs. Zungu, Mbaya's mother. What is the way forward for Mbaya from now?" the chief asked pointing at Mr. Kubwa, the elders' chairman.

"I agree with Mrs. Zungu. The community may not readily receive Mbaya among them with open arms. I live with a son who continues to limp due to injuries caused by Mbaya before rehab. Other members of the community whose items were stolen by Mbaya's gang and not paid for, are still bitter about Mbaya and his former comrades. I suggest the elders wisely approach Mr. Zungu, persuade him to receive back his son, Mbaya, as he has changed for the better. As you know, chief, Mr. Zungu and I disagree in almost everything. I know some elders Mr. Zungu might listen to. However, this process might take time. Meanwhile, Mbaya will need accommodation and a school to attend. What do other elders think about the problem?" Mr. Kubwa asked.

Another elder spoke up. "It will be necessary to call community meetings where Mbaya will give a testimony about his better behavior after rehab and apologize to the community for what he did before going to rehab. Mbaya's family will need to pay for the items stolen by Mbaya's gang before he went to rehab. This is likely to change the community's perception that Mbaya's old gang behavior has changed for the better. I agree with Mr. Kubwa, the elders' chair that this will take time."

"We still have no solution for Mbaya in spite of good testimonies about him and a very good report from CRC," the chief said.

For about three minutes after chief's comments, there was dead silence. The silence was followed by murmurs among those who attended the meeting but none of the community elders came up with a solution to Mbaya's problem. Meanwhile, the

Pastor, Caleb, and Mbaya conversed among themselves.

Caleb stood up. "Mr. Chief, chairman of community elders, Mrs. Zungu, and committee members, please allow me to make a few remarks concerning Mbaya. Since there is a problem of accommodating Mbaya either with his family or with the community, my father, the Pastor, and I have agreed to accommodate Mbaya at our home. By the way, Mbaya has been granted one year's scholarship by CRC for grade three next year."

"Wow! That's excellent! On behalf of everybody here and the Zungu family, accept our thanks for resolving Mbaya's problem," the Chief said.

The meeting ended at 4.00 p.m. The CRC driver drove to the Pastor's home where Caleb and Mbaya stayed until school opened the following year.

Mrs. Zungu's Report after Dinner

After the meeting at the chief's office, Mbaya's mother went home dejected. She wasn't sure how to tell her husband that Mbaya couldn't come home. Neither did she want to talk to any of her other children. She busied herself in the kitchen and made dinner of rice and chicken stew. The children always ate dinner in a different room from the parents. When dinner was ready at 7.00 p.m., Mrs. Zungu asked her husband to come for dinner, this time in the living room. As Mr. Zungu sat at the dining table, Mrs. Zungu brought in the three of Mbaya's siblings, an older brother and two younger sisters, to join them. Mrs. Zungu first served food to her husband, her oldest son and finally served the younger children. After dinner, they all started to drink hot tea with milk and sugar in it. As they were drinking tea, Mrs. Zungu stood up.

"The reason I called you here to eat together is because we are one family, including Mbaya who isn't with us. Today, I went to the chief's office where a meeting was held about Mbaya. In the presence of the chief, the elders' chairman, and other elders, we discussed Mbaya's CRC report about his good behavior since he went to rehab. A CRC pastor and his son narrated to us their personal testimony about Mbaya's good behavior when he spent a weekend with them at their home. It was a great moment for me. I was asked whether we were ready to receive Mbaya here at home since his behavior had changed for the better. In spite of motherly feelings for Mbaya, I declined on account of my husband's health and the fact that we are not ready for him. Furthermore, the community isn't ready to receive him. It's well known that Mbaya and his gang stole various items from members of this community. The elders at the meeting suggested that if we paid for the stolen items, the community might feel that Mbaya and his family are remorseful. It was also agreed that some elders will come to see

Mbaya's father, your father, and my husband, to discuss Mbaya's case concerning how to absorb him into the community," Mrs. Zungu sat down.

Neither Mr. Zungu nor Mbaya's siblings spoke a word for nearly five minutes. They all looked down after listening to Mrs. Zungu. Finally, Mr. Zungu spoke up.

"Let the children go to their rooms and sleep! Mbaya's matter is between you and me," Mr. Zungu told his wife.

"It's not right, my husband. Please, allow the kids to give us their input on how to deal with Mbaya when he comes home, if ever he does," pleaded Mrs. Zungu.

"Let them go and think about it. Kids, go to your rooms now!" Mr. Zungu thundered.

The three of Mr. and Mrs. Zungu's children rose up and quickly disappeared into their rooms without uttering a word.

Mr. Zungu turned and faced his wife. "As my wife and a Christian, you know you ought to obey me and not contradict me in the presence of our children. Why did you do it today?" Mr. Zungu asked.

In a humble and low quivering voice Mrs. Zungu replied, "Please, forgive me. It is my love for you and our children, including Mbaya that drove me to behave the way I did. I feel we are alienating our children from ourselves as parents. Mbaya is now like a prodigal son," Mrs. Zungu said.

"What! Mbaya doesn't deserve the respect of a prodigal son. He is a criminal. He made me have a heart attack because of his lies and criminal activities," Mr. Zungu replied to his wife.

"But he has changed for the better after rehab," replied Mrs. Zungu.

"I don't believe it. Three months in a rehab cannot change

Mbaya's criminal tendencies," Mr. Zungu told his wife.

"I saw our son, Mbaya, this afternoon in the chief's office. He has changed. Not the Mbaya you knew or described," Mrs. Zungu told her husband.

"What made you change your mind about Mbaya when you saw him? Mr. Zungu asked his wife.

"He was healthy, good looking, and respectful. He commended the elders for deciding to take him away to be rehabilitated, he apologized to us, his parents, and to the community for letting us down. Further, his good behavior and excellent academic performance at the CRC, won him a full year's tuition to a boarding school of his choice. Aren't these great achievements?" Mrs. Zungu asked her husband.

"Where did he go after the meeting at the chief's office?" Mr. Zungu asked his wife.

"He went with the CRC pastor who brought him to the meeting at the chief's office. You see, Mbaya is a great friend to one of the CRC pastor's son, Caleb. Next year, Mbaya will attend the same boarding school as Caleb. CRC pastor's family loves Mbaya according to what the pastor and his son said during the meeting," Mrs. Zungu replied to her husband.

"What you've told me is interesting. However, I don't want to see Mbaya in this family for a while. He will influence his siblings the wrong way and affect my health when I remember his behavior before rehab," Mr. Zungu told his wife.

"During the meeting at the chief's office," Mrs. Zungu told her husband, "the chief expressed great concern that we were not ready to receive our son back home. It was decided that some elders, apart from the elder's chairman, will come to see us to discuss how best to absorb Mbaya into the community."

"I look forward to seeing those elders and hearing their

advice. Mr. Kubwa, the elder's chairman, will not be welcome here. He demands that we pay hospital bills for Kogi's injury that was caused by Mbaya after school," Mr. Zungu told his wife.

"I agree with you. It's is hard for us. But I also think it might be one of the ways through which to regain trust from the community. Our son was the gang leader before he was sent to rehab," Mrs. Zungu told her husband.

"Well, let's wait and see," Mr. Zungu commented.

At 9.30 p.m. that evening, the Zungus retired to bed.

A week later, two of the community elders came to see Mr. and Mrs. Zungu. They knocked at Mr. Zungu's house door that led to the living room.

"Come on in. Good morning?" Mrs. Zungu said.

"Good morning, Mrs. Zungu," the two elders replied.

"Please, have a seat," Mrs. Zungu directed them to sit on a sofa.

"May I offer you tea or coffee?" Mrs. Zungu asked.

"Two cups of tea, please," the first elder replied.

Mrs. Zungu served the elders with hot cups of tea. As the elders drank tea, Mrs Zungu dashed to fetch Mr. Zungu.

"Hello, gentlemen!" Mr. Zungu said loudly.

"Hello, Mr. Zungu!" the two elders replied in unison.

"Welcome to our home. How may we help you?" Mr. Zungu asked.

"First, we want to thank Mrs. Zungu for receiving us so warmly with a cup of hot tea. Secondly, we are pleased to see you fully recovered from the heart attack. We also bring best wishes from the chief and the committee of the community elders," the first elder told Mr. and Mrs. Zungu.

"Thanks, you are welcome," Mr. Zungu replied.

"Another reason for coming to see you is because of your son, Mbaya, who finished his rehab at CRC," the second elder said.

"What about him?" Mr. Zungu asked.

"We saw him, heard from him, read reports about him from CRC rehab, and heard convincing testimonies about him from a CRC pastor and his son," the first elder replied.

"What was your conclusion about all this?" Mr. Zungu asked.

"That he is no longer the Mbaya we knew before he went to rehab, a gang leader. He is a well-behaved young man with incredible potential. We feel sorry that none of us offered to accommodate him. The CRC pastor took him back," the second elder said.

"Sorry I couldn't attend that meeting at the chief's office. My wife represented me. What do you want me to do about Mbaya?" Mr. Zungu asked the two elders.

"Well, the chief requires you and the elders' committee to have a meeting at his office Monday next week. We'll discuss the whole issue about Mbaya," the first elder replied.

"Will the elders' chairman, Mr. Kubwa, be in the meeting?" Mr. Zungu ask.

"No," the elders replied.

"In that case I'll attend the meeting. What time will the meeting be?" Mr. Zungu asked.

"The meeting will start at 9.00 a.m. and end before 11.00 a.m.," the second elder replied.

"Thanks," Mr. Zungu said.

"We do appreciate your hospitality this morning. See you at the meeting on Monday at 9.00 a.m.," the elders told Mr. and Mrs. Zungu.

As soon as the two elders left, Mr. Zungu asked his wife to call their three children to come to the living room. The children came quickly and stood in front of their parents looking scared. Mr. Zungu asked them to sit on the sofas.

"Are you ready to receive your brother, Mbaya, back home?" Mr. Zungu asked the children.

"No dad," replied the oldest son.

"Why?" Mr. Zungu asked his oldest son.

"There is much bitterness against Mbaya in the community. Kogi, his former classmate whom he hurt, along with his classmates, swear revenge on him. People in the community whose goods were stolen are demanding compensation," Mr. Zungu's oldest son replied.

"What about you two?" Mr. Zungu asked his two daughters.

"We agree with what our older brother has said," Zungu's two daughters replied in unison. In addition, they said, "We feel we need more freedom to express our ideas within our family. We feel caged. I think this is what led our brother, Mbaya, to misbehave as he tried to look for a way to express himself," Mr. Zungu's older daughter said.

Looking exasperated, Mr. Zungu told his oldest daughter, "That's enough! You may all leave the room now."

Mr. Zungu's oldest son and the two daughters hurried out of the room without knowing what their father would do next.

Compensation for Stolen and Damaged Goods

Mr. Zungu asked his wife, to accompany him to the meeting at the chief's office the following Monday. The committee of elders was led by their vice-chairman. The meeting was chaired by the chief.

The chief called the meeting to order, "Ladies and gentlemen, you know why I called this meeting. Two weeks ago, Mr. and Mrs. Zungu's son, Mbaya, was brought here after rehab. In spite of his good behavior that we witnessed and also read about from his CRC rehab reports, we failed to absorb him into the community, not even with his parents. Yet, as you know, he did so well at CRC that he secured one year's scholarship for his next class, and, in a boarding school. Mr. Zungu, don't you think you've abdicated your parental responsibility concerning your son, Mbaya?

"No," replied Mr. Zungu.

"Explain to this meeting why you think haven't neglected Mbaya, your son," the chief asked.

"My wife represented me in the meeting you held when Mbaya was brought from CRC. She gave plausible reasons why Mbaya couldn't come home. Additionally, if Mbaya came home, some people in the community might harm him because of his previous misdeeds," Mr. Zungu said.

"So, what is your long-term plan for Mbaya as a parent?" the chief asked.

"Well, while Mbaya is away, my wife and I have agreed to make good the damage he caused as a gang leader to individuals in the community. Hopefully, this will make the community feel we're remorseful," Mr. Zungu said.

"That sounds good. What do others think?" the chief asked.

"That is reasonable. We'll also need to make the community understand that Mbaya's behavior has changed for the better," the elders' spokesman replied.

"How will the community be made to understand that Mbaya is a changed young man?" the chief asked.

An elder in the meeting raised his hand, stood up, and said, "You, our chief should call public meetings at the shopping centers to explain to the people how Mbaya's behavior has changed since he went to rehab. It will also be necessary to read Mbaya's CRC reports to the people."

Another elder replied, "There is nothing more convincing than a personal testimony. Mbaya will need to come to the meetings for people to see him and answer their questions."

Mbaya's mother stood up, "I don't want my son to appear in the community meetings for security reasons. He will also be humiliated."

The chief tapped the table with his hand to draw attention to all in the meeting. "Let's start with what we can accomplish quickly. After all, schools have opened and we don't want to interrupt Mbaya from his school work. We will start by paying the owners of the items stolen or damaged by Mbaya and his gang before he went to rehab. The amount is $100.00. Additionally, Mbaya caused great harm to Kogi, his classmate. He injured one of his legs and tore his clothes and books on that terrible afternoon as they went home from school. According to Mr. Kubwa, the elders' chairman, the total amount, including the hospital bill is $150.00. Mr. and Mrs. Zungu will pay the $150.00 to Mr. Kubwa."

"That's too much money! I'll not pay until I've ascertained the amount from the hospital where Kubwa's son was treated," Mr. Zungu said.

"Here are the receipts of the doctors's bills paid by Mr. Kubwa after his son was treated at the hospital. I agree. It's prudent to verify the authenticity of the receipts," the chief replied.

"Who will pay the $ 100.00 remaining?" Mrs. Zungu asked.

"The parents of the three boys who were Mbaya's accomplices during the night raid in the community," the chief replied.

"When and where will the money be paid?" the elders' spokesman asked.

"The money must be paid before the end of this month here in my office. My office will make sure everyone pays on time. After receiving it, I will call a meeting of all concerned to ensure they receive their dues," the chief replied.

All the elders in the meeting clapped to show their agreement with the chief's decision.

"Do you have any more comments or questions?" the chief asked.

"No!" the elders replied in unison.

But Mr. and Mrs. Zungu remained quiet.

At the end of the month, the chief received the money from the parents of Mbaya's accomplices, a total of $100.00. Mr. Zungu, Mbaya's father hadn't paid the $150.00 he was supposed to pay. The chief was about to send policemen to bring Mr. Zungu to his office when his secretary called.

"Hello sir, Mr. Zungu wants to see you," the secretary said.

"Let him come to my office," the chief replied.

The secretary asked Mr. Zungu to record his name, his identity number, and time-in in a register that lay on her desk. She gave Mr. Zungu a pass to enter the chief's office. At the door of the chief's office was a guard who vetted people before entering the office.

"Hello sir! Can I help you?" the guard asked Mr. Zungu.

"I just want to see the chief," Mr. Zungu replied.

"Give me the pass you got from the secretary," the guard demanded.

Mr. Zungu searched for the pass from his trousers' pockets, then from his jacket's pockets, and finally from his brief case but couldn't find it.

"I don't seem to have it. The chief knows me. Can I get in?" Mr. Zungu said impatiently.

"No sir. Please, get another pass from the secretary," the guard replied.

Looking angry and embarrassed, Mr. Zungu went to retrieve the pass from the trash can where he had thrown it.

"Go in sir," the guard opened the door for Mr. Zungu to see the chief.

"Good morning Mr. Zungu?" the chief said.

"Good morning chief," replied Mr. Zungu.

"Please, have a seat," the chief said to Mr. Zungu as he showed him where to sit.

"I'm sorry chief for not paying the $150.00 earlier. I had to verify that the receipts from Mr. Kubwa were genuine. I'll pay the money though I'm not sure that some of the receipts are correct," Mr. Zungu told the chief.

"Pay the money now and discuss any discrepancies with Mr. Kubwa later," the chief told Mr. Zungu.

The chief's office cashier took the money from Mr. Zungu

and issued him a receipt.

"Thank you, Mr. Zungu for fulfilling your commitment. Please, follow me," the chief told Mr. Zungu. He opened a door that led to a hall. The hall had four large windows fitted with wooden shutters that were fully open to allow day light in. In the middle of the hall were forty plastic chairs arranged in four rows. In front of the chairs was a table beside which were three wooden chairs. The chief and the cashier sat on two wooden chairs beside the table. Mr. Zungu sat on one of the plastic chairs in the front row among other elders who had come in earlier.

"How are you gentlemen?" the chief said as he waved at the elders.

"We are fine," the elders replied in unison.

"As you know, I asked you to come here to be paid for some of the damages caused by Mbaya and his accomplices on the night they invaded your homes. Mbaya had also seriously injured Kubwa's son, Kogi, the day before the night of invasion. I would like you to understand that nobody can pay you for the psychological pain and trauma you experienced, and, perhaps are still experiencing due to that horrible night. I hope this payment will help begin to improve relationships among yourselves and the people in the community," the chief told the elders.

The chief called out the names of those to be paid. Two men received $40.00 each and one man received $20. They signed their names in a register maintained by the cashier after receiving the money.

"Mr. Kubwa, chairman of the elders' committee, please, come forward!" the chief said.

Mr. Kubwa came forward and stood beside the chief and faced the elders in the hall.

"I want to thank the Chief for calling us to be paid for the damages and for the things stolen by the gang of boys on that terrible night. My son, Kogi, was seriously injured by Mbaya as they came from school and still limps due to that injury. In another incident that I hope Mr. Zungu can recall, Mbaya harassed and splashed water on Kogi at the river when Kogi was drawing water for his grandmother. Also, as you know Chief, Mr. Zungu is the deputy chairman of the elders' committee. He and I hold opposite views concerning how to solve problems in our community and our families. Nonetheless, I respect him. I, therefore, respectfully decline to receive the $150.00 from him though it is due to me. I suggest that he uses the money to help Mbaya," Mr. Kubwa said.

Mr. Zungu stood up and said, "Chief, I respect Mr. Kubwa as the chairman of the elders' committee. But, why didn't he report to me that my son, Mbaya, harassed Kogi, his son, in the drawing water incident?"

"Mr. Kubwa, why didn't you? The chief asked

"Chief, Mr. Zungu's son, Comba, stopped Mbaya from causing more trouble for Kogi. Comba came to me and apologized on behalf of Mbaya. His apology was enough. I also assumed Comba informed his father about Mbaya's misbehavior against Kogi. It's also generally known in our community that Mr. Zungu doesn't like people who have less education than he, especially, if they are business people. His home and mine are close to each other, yet, we hardly discuss any issues," Mr. Kubwa said.

"Mr. Zungu, you are the vice-chairman to Mr. Kubwa, the community chairman. You both should be working together for the benefit of the community notwithstanding your personal differences," the Chief said looking at Mr. Kubwa and Mr. Zungu.

Mr. Kubwa nodded in agreement with the Chief but Mr. Zungu shrugged and looked away from the Chief.

The Chief called off the meeting and the elders went away.

Kogi's School Progress and Reactions

Mbaya's attack on Kogi a year ago left Kogi with a scar and a limp on his left leg.

"I need to teach Mbaya a lesson for hurting me so badly. I understand that he is in a boarding school far away from our community. Somehow, he will pay for what he did to me?" Kogi thought to himself.

Meanwhile, Kogi's dad came in. It was supper time and Kogi's mom had prepared a delicious meal. She served food to her husband and asked her children to serve themselves. As was custom in Kubwa's family, the day's happenings were discussed after supper.

"How was your day?" Kubwa asked Kogi.

"It was great. I'm doing very well in my school work. I hope to go to one of the best national high schools in the country," Kogi told his father.

"Excellent! A boarding school would be good for you. Wouldn't it? Kubwa asked.

"Yes dad. I'll learn to be independent and make new friends," Kogi replied.

"Would you like to go to the same high school as Mbaya? It's a great school. This might help you reconcile with Mbaya," Kubwa asked.

Kogi's mom who eagerly listened to the discussion between father and son interjected.

"That is an excellent idea for you, Kogi, to reconcile with Mbaya while still in school. Mbaya's mom told me that Mbaya has changed for the better and wishes to meet you," Kogi's mom said.

"Please, mom and dad, I'm still suffering from mental anguish and physical scars inflicted by Mbaya. I don't want to be in the same school with him. Perhaps later in life we might be reconciled if things go well between us," Kogi told his parents.

"I understand what you feel about Mbaya because of the way he bullied and hurt you. Mbaya's father, paid me $150.00 for medical and other expenses incurred because of your injury. I declined and asked him to use it toward helping Mbaya. Good relations in the community are better than money," Kubwa told his son.

"But why doesn't Mbaya's dad like us though we are good neighbors in the community?" Kogi asked his parents.

"Perhaps he is embarrassed because Mbaya didn't turn out to be what he wanted him to be in spite of his strict Christian discipline," Kubwa replied.

"You are correct dad. That's what most people in the community think about Mr. Zungu. Nonetheless, as a Christian and a teacher, he should treat other people like he would like to be treated," Kogi told his dad.

"Well son, even as Christians, we need to have wisdom to put the Christian principles into action in ways that are beneficial to us and other people, especially our families. As you know, the church we attend is different from Mr. Zungu's church," Kubwa told his son Kogi.

"Dad, I love the way you allow us to discuss things every time after dinner. Many of my school mates don't discuss their problem with their parents. They fear them. Nonetheless, going to the same high school as Mbaya isn't good for me," Kogi told his dad.

"Okay, it is your choice," Kubwa told his son.

"My class teacher recommended that I choose the best national high school because I have always scored "As" in all subjects in my school," Kogi informed his dad.

"That is very wise. When will you make the choice for the high school you intend to attend?" Kubwa asked his son.

"I have made a tentative choice to go to the top high school in the nation. However, acceptance to this top high school is dependent on how well I perform in the final national examination that will take place in one months' time," Kogi told his dad.

"Are you prepared for the national examination?" Kubwa asked his son.

"Yes dad. At school our teachers are reviewing with us relevant materials related to the examination. Additionally, four of us have formed a study group in which we review our class notes, text book materials, ask each other questions, and share our knowledge with each other. This is in addition to individual private studies," Kogi answered his dad.

"Wonderful and best of luck!" Kubwas replied to his son.

Two weeks before the national examination took place, Kogi went to school as usual. Out of 30 students in his class only 15 were present. Apparently, the absent students thought it more productive to work from home rather than come to school. They had become extremely jittery due to the upcoming national examination. To help reduce examination nervousness and fear, the school's head teacher arranged that the following Friday be a day of prayer for the students doing the national examination.

On the national examination day, the candidates gathered in

the school hall which had ample space. Each student sat on a chair in front of which was a desk bearing the student's examination number. The space between one student and the next was about six feet. This was to ensure that there was no interference between students during the examination. After the students settled down and sat on their chairs, the invigilator rang the bell,

"Listen up students! I will supply you with question papers. Below each question is a space to write answers. Any questions?" the invigilator asked.

A hand shot up.

"Suppose the space below the question is not enough for my answers. What shall I do?" one student asked.

"You will raise up your hand and I will supply you with more paper for your answers," the invigilator replied.

"Listen up again! After you get your questions, I will give you five minutes to read through. During that time you are not allowed to write anything but to read and point out what you don't understand. After five minutes, I will ring the bell for all to start writing answers to the questions. You will raise up your hand if you have a question," the invigilator said.

There were no hands raised and the invigilator continued,

"Ten minutes to the hour, I will ring the bell as a warning for you to finish writing. Finally I'll ring the bell for everybody to stop writing. If you continue writing after the final bell, I will destroy your papers. Any questions?" the invigilator asked.

The examination for the English grammar started immediately since there were no questions asked. When the final bell was rung, majority of the students stopped writing. One student went on writing after hearing the final bell. The invigilator looked at him, slowly moved toward him, grabbed his answer papers, tore them into shreds and tossed them into the trash bin. It was a very frightening experience to the rest of the students. One by one, students placed the examination papers on the invigilator's desk and went out of the hall for a short break. At 11.00 a.m., the students returned to the examination hall. The invigilator gave similar instructions he had given in the first examination after which the examination for English composition commenced and went on till 12.00 noon. Thereafter, students were released to go home since there were no examinations in the afternoon. Examinations for mathematics, geography, history and civics were done in the second day. Finally, science, art and music examinations were done in the third day. Before the students left for their homes, the invigilator wished them a merry Christmas as they waited for their examination results.

In the first week of January the following year, Kogi bumped into his primary school teacher.

"Hello Kogi!" the teacher said.

"Hello sir!" Kogi replied.

"Have you heard the news?" the teacher asked.

"Which news sir?" Kogi asked.

"Well, your national examination results are out. Go to school and ask the head teacher for your grades," the teacher advised Kogi.

That same day, Kogi contacted Kega, his friend and classmate.

"Our national examination results are out. Tomorrow we must go and see the head teacher for our grades," Kogi told Kega.

"Of course! Shall we go in the morning or afternoon?" Kega asked.

"Definitely in the morning," Kogi replied.

The following day, Kogi and Kega went to school to get their examination results. At 8.00 o'clock in the morning, they sat on a bench outside the head teacher's office.

"Hi boys! Come on in and have a seat. How are you doing after your examination?" the head teacher asked.

"We've been helping our parents in their domestic chores while eagerly waiting for our examination grades," Kogi and Kega replied.

"How do you think you did in your national examination?" the head teacher asked.

"We think we did well but we can't be sure until we see the results," Kogi and Kega replied.

The head teacher opened his filing cabinet and took out two documents: a list of names with respective grades written against each name.

"Kogi, you did us proud! You got straight "As" in all the subjects. Congratulations! Kega you also did us proud! You got five straight "As" and one "B+." Congratulations! You two are the best in your class," the head teacher said.

"We thank you very much, sir, for all you did to enable us do so well in the national examination," Kogi and Kega told the head teacher.

"Excuse me sir. Which was subject that I got a "B+"?" Kega asked the head teacher.

"Art and music. That shouldn't worry you as I will explain to you shortly," The head teacher told Kega.

"What are our chances of going to the premier national high school?" Kogi asked the head teacher.

The head teacher smiled broadly, looked at his watch and said,

"Both of you have been selected to go to the premier national high school. These are your letters of admission to the school," the head teacher told Kogi and Kega.

"Wow! Wow! This is unbelievable!" Kogi exclaimed.

"It is a dream come true, Kogi!" Kega exclaimed.

The head teacher stood up and hugged Kogi and Kega. He gave each of them the letter of admission from the premier national high school.

"Read the letter, show it to your parents and discuss with them. Ensure you adhere to all the requirements mentioned in the letter of admission and report to the school as instructed. If you encounter any difficulties, let me know. Okay?" The head teacher said.

"Yes and thank you sir," Kogi and Kega replied and went home.

Mbaya's Life after Rehab

"Hello Mbaya! Welcome back to the family," Caleb's mother told Mbaya.

"Thank you very much mom," Mbaya replied.

During supper, Caleb's brother and sisters were curious to see Mbaya back at their home. After all, their dad and the CRC Rehab driver had taken him back to his parents.

"I'm sure you are eager to know why Mbaya is here with us and didn't go to his parents," the Pastor said.

"Yes, we are but glad to have Mbaya back in our home. All the same, tell us what happened when you took him back to his parents," Caleb's mother asked her husband.

"We were very well received by the chief's officers and the chief himself. Mbaya's mother and the community leaders were present in the meeting. The chief called the meeting to order. After brief introductions, Mbaya's CRC report was read and discussed. Caleb and I were asked to give testimonies to support that Mbaya had changed for the better. The chief and some elders asked Mbaya questions about his life at the CRC Rehab. Mbaya apologized for his previous misdeeds in the community and then answered the questions admirably. The chief and the elders were convinced that Mbaya had changed for the better after rehab. Mbaya's mother stood up, moved closer to Mbaya, and, weeping hugged him," the Pastor narrated.

"What followed?" Caleb's mother asked.

"Mbaya's mother said that her husband was unwell. Since Mbaya and his father don't see eye-to-eye, it would be counter-productive for Mbaya to come home at this time. Also, the community is anti-Mbaya at this juncture. This isn't the right time for him to come home. That's why Mbaya came back with us," the Pastor said.

"Welcome back to the family," Caleb's big brother told Mbaya.

"Yes, welcome back and feel at home," Caleb's sisters said in unison.

The Pastor stood up, laid his hands on Mbaya's head. He said a prayer to thank God for Mbaya's return to their home and for a safe journey to and fro. Everybody said Amen after the prayer.

"Well, we've only one month before schools open. Which school will Mbaya attend?" Caleb's big brother asked.

"He and I will go to the same school, but of course, we'll be in different classes; he will be in grade three and I in grade seven. I'll protect him from bullies," Caleb said.

"That's a great answer Caleb. Mbaya will stay with us until he finishes school or until his parents come for him and he chooses to go with them," the Pastor said.

"Clap! Clap! Clap!" the Pastor's family clapped in agreement.

Mbaya stood up with tears of joy flowing on his cheeks and said,

"Thank you very much for loving me so much. You have taught me how to be a Christian though I was born by Christian parents. You have encouraged and made me discover my potential. You have accepted me in your home while I'm rejected by my own family and community. May God bless you."

It was time to go to bed. Caleb accommodated Mbaya in his visitors' bed. But before going to bed, Mbaya discussed with Caleb as follows,

"Would you mind if you and I looked after the cows before school opens next month?" Mbaya asked Caleb.

"That's a brilliant idea. Let's discuss it with mom and dad tomorrow during breakfast," Caleb replied.

During breakfast the following morning, Caleb approached his dad and mom and said, "Mbaya and I would like to be allocated one area of work in our homestead to which we will accountable. We will help in other areas but only after we finish working in our area of work. I hope this isn't asking too much from you dad and mom."

Caleb's dad and mom consulted each other after which Caleb's dad said, "That's a great request. Before you go back to school next month, we want you to look after the cows. This means that you will be waking up at 6.00 in the morning. You will milk the cows, weigh the milk, ensure that the milk is taken to the dairy, and feed the cows before you come for breakfast. During the day, you will let the cows out of their pens to graze in various paddocks within the homestead. Watch out for sick cows or cows on heat and call the vet to fix the problems. Do you have any questions?" Caleb's dad asked.

"No dad, that's great" Caleb replied to his dad.

After breakfast, Caleb and Mbaya went to find out how many cows were in milk.

"Hi gentlemen!" Caleb said to the employee-milkmen.

"Hi Caleb! What can we do for you?" one milkman replied.

"How many cows did you milk this morning?" Caleb asked.

"Five," the second milkman replied.

"That means five other cows aren't in milk," Caleb asked.

"Yes, but they are in calf," the first milkman replied.

"How long before they produce the calves?" Mbaya asked the second milkman.

"Four months," the second milkman replied.

"Wow! That means you will be milking ten cows every morning. Will you manage to milk all of them?" Caleb asked.

"Of course, we will manage. We'll start milking at 6 a.m. instead of 7 a.m.," the milkmen replied to Caleb.

"That's great! Tomorrow we'll join you in milking and looking after the cows. By the way, this is Mbaya, my friend," Caleb told the milkmen.

The following morning, Caleb and Mbaya woke up earlier than usual and arrived the cow sheds at 6 a.m. As soon the cows saw them, they raised their heads up and mooed. The cows in milk darted toward the milking pens.

"Oh, oh, what does this mean?" Caleb asked Mbaya.

"Let's get some hay and put it in the troughs. This will keep the cows silent as they eat the hay. Meanwhile we'll clean the udders and teats of the cows to be milked," Mbaya told Caleb."

"I haven't milked for a long time. I'll watch as you milk and help in any other way you tell me," Caleb told Mbaya.

"Okay, watch out how I clean my hands before milking. Please, pass to me that clean ten pound bucket for putting the milk," Mbaya said.

Mbaya placed the bucket under the cow's teats.

"Pass the stool to me and watch," Mbaya told Caleb.

Mbaya sat on the stool next to the cow. With his two hands firmly holding the cow's teats, he squeezed out milk from all the teats until no more milked came out.

"Wow! You are an expert milker," Caleb told Mbaya.

At 7 a.m. when the two employee-milkers arrived, two cows had been milked by Mbaya. The milkers were puzzled at the turn of events.

"Don't worry just milk the remaining cows," Caleb told the milkers.

"Can I milk a third cow?" Mbaya asked Caleb.

"Oh yes, go ahead," Caleb replied.

At 7.30 a.m., all the five cows had been milked. Each milker weighed his milk before it was taken to the dairy.

"The total quantity of milk from the three cows I milked is 83 pounds," Mbaya reported to Caleb.

"The total quantity from the two cows we milked is 50 pounds," the two employee-milkers reported to Caleb.

"That means all the milk for today weighs 133 pounds," Caleb said.

"That is correct, puzzling, and interesting. We have always averaged 125 pounds a day from the five cows. How come we have a difference of 8 pounds today?" one employee-milker asked.

"We'll discuss the discrepancy tomorrow morning as we weigh the milk. Look over there. The dairy truck has come to pick up the milk," Caleb said.

The employee-milkmen loaded three 50 pounds milk cans on to the truck after which the truck sped out of the homestead.

"Thank you all. You can now go for your breakfast," Caleb said.

At 10 am, Caleb and Mbaya went back to the cows' sheds. The employee-milkers were busy cleaning the cow sheds and troughs.

Each employee-milker wore an overall, a pair of gumboots, a pair of gloves, and a hat. Using a shovel, they scooped cow's dung from the floor and put it on wheelbarrows. When the wheelbarrows were full, they wheeled them out and dumped out the contents. It took an hour to clean the cow sheds and the troughs.

"That's great work you've done," Caleb told the employee-milkers.

"Thanks. You see, clean sheds and troughs prevent various diseases from affecting the cows. The cows also feel comfortable and produce more milk," one employee-milker told Caleb and Mbaya.

"Very good. We'll take the cows to graze in the paddocks. This will give you enough time to finish cleaning and prepare for milking at 6 p.m.," Caleb told the employee-milkers.

"Great! We'll meet at 6 pm for milking," both employee-milkers responded.

"Okay," Caleb said.

Caleb and Mbaya let the cows out of the sheds and drove them toward the paddocks. A few cows broke out of the herd and ran away from the direction of the paddocks. Mbaya ran and redirected them to the rest of the herd and in to the paddocks.

"Look over there. There is a lot of dry hay spread out on the ground. The grass growing in the paddock is lush and green. Should we allow the cows to feed first on hay or the lush green grass?" Caleb asked Mbaya.

"We'll first feed them on hay," Mbaya replied.

"Why?" Caleb asked Mbaya.

"Because green grass is tender and palatable, cows tend to eat a lot of it. This makes the cows produce much gas in their stomachs resulting in bloating, a condition that may result in death. When the cows eat dry hay followed by green grass, the chances of bloating become much less," Mbaya answered Caleb.

"What an excellent explanation! From where did you learn all this?" Caleb asked.

"I learned it from the old men with whom I herded cattle. The knowledge was passed to them by their grandfathers," Mbaya answered Caleb.

"What a legacy!" Caleb exclaimed.

It was about 6 p.m. when Caleb and Mbaya drove the cows back to the cow sheds for milking.

"The cows look very well fed. Look at how big their stomachs are!" one employee-milker exclaimed.

"This evening milk production will be higher than usual," the second milker said.

"Let your friend, Mbaya, milk three cows and we'll milk the other two," one milker told Caleb.

"That's fine with me," Caleb replied.

"Our two milkers request that you milk three cows this evening. Is that okay?" Caleb asked Mbaya.

"Oh yes. As a matter of fact, I can milk all the five cows if need be," Mbaya replied.

That evening, Mbaya milked three cows while the two employee-milkers milked two. Normally, the five cows produced 135 pounds of milk every evening, an average of 27 pounds per cow. That evening, the two cows produced 55 pounds, an average of 27.5 pounds per cow milked by employee-milkers. The three cows milked by Mbaya produced 91 pounds, an average 30.3 pounds per cow. Thus, there was an increase of 2% in milk production from cows milked by employee-milkers compared to the normal average weight. Also, there was an increase of 12% in milk production from three cows milked by Mbaya.

"Well, well, we need to discuss why Mbaya is able to produce more milk than each one of you," Caleb told the employee-milkers.

"Okay, let's put the milk in the freezer then we can discuss the issue," the employee-milkers said.

"It's important to ensure you spend enough time on each cow to squeeze out all the milk through the teats. When a cow being milked finishes eating the feeds in the trough, it becomes agitated and tends to kick about with its hind legs. Milk disappears from its teats. Putting more feeds in the trough calms the cow as it eats. Milk starts flowing through the teats again. That's why you find that I'm always last when milking. Try this technique next time when you are milking," Mbaya said.

"We will," the employee-milkers replied.

"Good! Today we've done very well resulting in increased milk production. Congratulations to all of us!" Caleb exclaimed.

Caleb and Mbaya went home and took a shower, changed their clothes, and joined the other members of the family for supper.

"What's up you two guys?" Caleb's mother asked.

"We feel great but we are physically tired," Caleb replied to his mother.

"Okay. Eat your supper and we'll discuss the day's happenings as we drink coffee and tea," Caleb's mother said.

They sat on sofas in the living room, and, everybody waited expectantly to hear what Caleb and Mbaya did during the day.

Except Caleb, his father and mother, other members of the family knew precious little about cows.

"Did you enjoy looking after the cows?" Caleb's mother asked Mbaya.

"Yes mom," Mbaya replied.

"Mom, Mbaya is an expert in feeding and milking cows. Today I learned a great deal about cows from Mbaya," Caleb told his mom.

"Tell us more about what you learned," Caleb's older brother, Paul asked.

"The paddocks have lush with green grass. When cows eat the lush green grass, they are likely to develop excessive gas in their stomachs and cause bloating. That excessive gas may kill them in minutes. To prevent bloating, the cows should first be fed with dry hay. This is why the employee-milkers spread hay in the paddocks for cows to eat before feeding on the lush green grass.

"Wow! That is very insightful. When we started keeping cows, two of them died after grazing on green lush grass," Caleb's older brother, Paul said.

"That's correct. I urge each one of you to take interest in our cows. After all, the sale of milk contributes to the family budget," Caleb's mother told her children.

"Further, our two employee-milkers increased the milk output by 2% this evening. They milked two cows. Mbaya increased the output by 12% from the three cows he milked," Caleb said.

"Incredible! Congratulations! Let's all clap for Mbaya," Caleb's mom said.

"Oh yes, it's incredible. None of us, including our employee-milkers, would have guessed what to do to increase milk output.

I'll let Mbaya explain it to you," Caleb said.

"Thank you, Caleb. When milking, it's important to ensure that there is sufficient feed in the trough. As the cow continues to eat, milk flows readily from its teats. If the feedstuff finishes, the cow starts to kick about with its hind feet. This behavior reduces or stops milk flow from the cow's teats. It's also advisable to ensure that no milk is left in the cow's udder. In other words, don't rush when you start milking," Mbaya said.

"That's great! We can increase milk output if we follow Mbaya's advice. Anything else to teach this family?" Caleb asked Mbaya.

"Not really, except that cow sheds and the milking equipment should be kept clean. Milkers should wash their hands thoroughly and the cow's udder including the teats. This will reduce milk contamination," Mbaya said.

"What a good and productive evening we've had," Caleb's mom said.

"It's exciting and insightful. I propose that we learn how to look after the cows and how to milk," Caleb's older brother, Paul said.

"That's a great idea, Paul. However, remember we've three weeks before schools open, and, all of you will go to school. We must act fast. Paul, this week you will work at the cows with Caleb, Mbaya, and the milkers. Next week, these two girls, your sisters will work at the cows also. Learn all you can about the cows during your time there," Caleb's mom said.

Caleb's dad, the Pastor, arrived just after his children left the living room. He had a long day at church where he attended an annual church general meeting.

"I'm sorry to be so late. Church annual general meetings

tend to be too long. This is because committee reports must be discussed and questions from church members answered," The Pastor said.

"You must be starving?" Caleb's mom asked her husband, the Pastor.

"Not really. We had a Pastors' dinner at church," the Pastor answered.

"Hey, what is going on with Mbaya and Caleb and their work at the cows?" the Pastor asked.

"Great! Mbaya taught us how to look after the cows to increase milk production. Milk production rose by 12% from cows milked by Mbaya and 2% from cows milked by the regular milkers. He explained to us how cows should be fed when they are taken to the paddocks, how to milk to increase milk production, and to keep cow sheds clean. When you have time, it would be good for you to congratulate him on his good performance," Caleb's mom explained to her husband, the Pastor.

"That's great news. It's unfortunate that Mbaya's parents couldn't recognize his potential. I hope one day I'll be able to convince them that their son is a great one," the Pastor told his wife.

"If they don't want him, we'll adopt him to be our third son. What do you think?" Caleb's mom asked her husband, the Pastor.

"No objection but let's first deal with Mbaya's parents, especially his father, to understand what his plans are for Mbaya," The Pastor replied.

"There's another point we need to discuss concerning Mbaya's education. We know he got a scholarship for his grade three education. Who will pay tuition for his education further on?" Caleb's mom asked.

"That's a good question. I discussed Mbaya's plight with the church elders before we took him back to his parents and community who rejected him," the Pastor said.

"What did the elders say about him?" Caleb's mom asked.

"Some elders wanted the church to pay for his education all through to university. However, two church elders said the church shouldn't be burdened with Mbaya's problem. They were prepared to pay for his education and living expenses as long as he was in school. When we took a vote, the two elders won," the Pastor said.

"That's great for Mbaya," Caleb's mom said.

"Make sure you don't tell any of our children or Mbaya what we've discussed tonight," the Pastor told his wife.

The following morning, Paul, Caleb, and Mbaya went to milk at 6 am. They found that the employee-milkers had cleaned the feeding troughs and waited for them.

"Good morning gentlemen?" the employee-milkers said.

"Good morning. Did you sleep well?" Paul asked.

"Very well indeed," the employee-milkers replied.

"I have come so that you may teach me how to milk and to look after the cows. Is that okay with you?" Paul asked.

"Yes, we'll teach you what we know. Mbaya will teach you as well," the employee-milkers said.

"This is excellent. All we need for milking is ready. However, we need to wash the hands with hot water. Watch what I do. After washing the hands, smear this special lotion on the hands and the cow's teats. The lotion makes the teats pliable and prevents hurting them as milk is squeezed out," Mbaya explained.

As Mbaya milked three cows, Paul, Caleb, and the two employee-milkers watched what he did. It took Mbaya forty-five minutes to milk. Then it was the employee-milkers' turn to do the milking of the remaining two cows. It took thirty minutes to milk after which the milk was weighed.

"Look at the scale! Mbaya's milk weighs 92 pounds. Compare this with 81 pounds, the normal output for the three cows he milked. The employee-milkers' output from the two cows is 60 pounds. Compare this with 54 pounds, the normal weight of milk for the two cows. It all works out to an output increase of 14% and 11% respectively. This is outstanding work! Caleb said.

At 8.00 am, the dairy truck arrived and picked up the milk for delivery to the dairy. The employee-milkers went to their quarters while Paul, Caleb and Mbaya went to shower and breakfast.

"Hi guys! I didn't see you last night because I came late. How are you doing at the cows?" the Pastor asked Caleb, and Mbaya.

"We are doing great! Paul joined us today and we think he learned a lot this morning. Isn't it Paul?" Caleb asked.

"Yes I did, but there is much more to learn about cows. By the way dad, Caleb, Mbaya, and the employee-milkers have done incredible work. Milk output has increased by more than 10% of the normal output," Paul told his dad.

"How come the regular milkers produced less milk before Mbaya came?" the Pastor asked.

"They spent less time in milking, meaning that milk was left in the cows. This happened because when cows finished eating the feed in the trough, they got agitated and kicked their hind legs and milking stopped," Caleb explained to his dad.

"Have they been taught the new milking method?" The pastor asked.

"Oh yes. Their output has improved by a lot. Mbaya has been teaching them and they are doing very well," Caleb replied.

The Pastor stood up, approached Mbaya, hugged and patted him at the back.

"Thank you very much for the great work you've done in this family. May God richly bless you in the coming days," the Pastor said.

"I'm truly grateful for all you are doing for me," Mbaya said in tears.

"Thank you very much dad for congratulating Mbaya. He is a very resourceful member of our family," Caleb said.

"I'm pleased by your mom's plan for each of you to work at the cows. Mbaya and Caleb will teach you about milking and looking after cows before you go back to school," The Pastor told his children.

The following week, Caleb's two sisters joined Caleb, Mbaya, and the two employee-milkers at the cows. The sisters wore gumboots, old jeans, blouses, and tied headscarfs around their heads.

"Come nearer and watch how milking is done," Caleb told his two sisters.

"This place is too smelly. I don't think we can work here," the older sister told Caleb.

"Well, mom said you must learn how to milk and to look after the cows. Don't you recall?" Caleb asked his two sisters.

"We recall but mom can give us other types of work in the compound. This work is for you boys," Caleb's older sister said.

As Caleb's older sister was approaching the milking pen, she stepped on soft cow dung, slipped and fell backwards on more cow dung on the floor. She screamed. The two employee-milkers ran quickly and picked her up to her feet.

"Thank you for helping me to stand up on my feet," Caleb's older sister told the employee-milkers.

The two sisters walked away back home. They showered, put on their dresses, and went to see their mom.

"Hi girls! Didn't you go to work at the cows with Caleb and Mbaya?" Caleb's mom asked.

"Yes, we did mom. We didn't like working there. It's smelly and dangerous for us. Give us another chore in the house or outside the house," the two sisters told their mom.

"I'll think about it after I hear from Caleb and Mbaya when they come," Caleb's mom replied.

Caleb and Mbaya came back to the house after milking and feeding the cows.

"Hey mom, guess how much milk we got this morning?" Caleb asked.

"I'm not good at guessing. Perhaps Paul who worked at the cows last week might guess correctly," Caleb's mom said.

"Well, well, I think you got 150 pounds of milk this morning," Paul said.

"That was a good guess but we got 167 pounds. Mbaya's output was 105 pounds, an increase of 24% above normal output and employee-milkers' output was 62 pounds, an increase of 15% above normal output," Caleb said.

"Wow! That is highly commendable. I'm pleased to see that you're training the employee-milkers and that they are getting it," Caleb's mom said.

"Our employee-milkers are highly motivated. They follow Mbaya's milking instructions scrupulously. They are likely to increase milk production by 30% when we leave and go back to school. What do you think, Mbaya?" Caleb asked.

"You are correct, Caleb. However, I think if they're given incentives, they could increase milk production by 50%," Mbaya said.

"You mean we could be selling to the dairy four full 50 pounds cans of milk every day?" Caleb's mom asked.

"Yes, mom. You have great milk cows," Mbaya answered.

"That's very insightful, Mbaya," Caleb's mom said.

"What happened to our sisters when they came to work at the cows this morning?" Paul asked.

"When they arrived at the cows, they found us starting to milk. They stood far from the milking pens. My older sister started to complain about bad smell. As she was moving away from the cow sheds, she stepped on wet cow dung and fell backwards on more cow dung. The employee-milkers lifted her up to her feet. Both sisters immediately came back home," Caleb said.

"That explains it. Your dad and I will deal with them," Caleb's mom said.

"Mom, this is our last week to work at the cows before we go to school. My sisters lost their opportunity to learn how to milk and look after the cows," Caleb said.

"Certainly, they will regret it in the future," Caleb's mom said.

That week, Caleb and Mbaya discussed many issues with the employee-milkers as they worked at the cows.

"We have enjoyed working with you and learned a great deal about cows since we came here. I hope you also learned something from us?" Caleb asked the employee-milkers.

"Absolutely, we have learned a lot. Mbaya has revolutionized our milking methods resulting in increased milk output. You are good people with whom we talk and share ideas freely. We also feel you have seen the challenges we face as cattle herders. Caleb, please, talk to your parents to help us improve cattle rearing in general," the employee-milkers said.

"Thank you for your good comments. I'll talk to my parents about what is to be done for you and the improvement of the cows' facilities. However, ensure you continue to increase milk production. Aim at increasing milk production by 30% before the end of the month. Do you agree?" Caleb asked.

"We do, thanks," the employee-milkers said.

"Great! I would also like to inform you that this is our last week with you here at the cows. Next week we shall be preparing for school which opens next month. We hope to hear about your progress from dad and mom when they visit us at school. Best of luck," Caleb said.

Caleb and Mbaya Prepare for School

One evening after supper, the Pastor and his family were having coffee and tea in the living room. Caleb and Mbaya had worked for a month at the cows. They shared their findings before they went to school the following week.

"We had a fabulous time working with the employee-milkers at the cows. Through Mbaya and the employee-milkers, I learned how to milk and feed the cows for increased milk output. I also learned that cleanliness of the milkers, cows, and cow sheds is essential to prevent diseases and milk contamination," Caleb said.

"That is excellent Caleb. Everybody here should know how to milk and feed the cows," the Pastor said.

"We also found that some parts of the cow sheds have holes on the floor where concrete is broken. These holes make it difficult to clean the floor. Additionally, some of the milking pens need to be repaired. Further, the workers at the cows need to be given some incentives if we expect more increases in milk production. They agreed to increase milk output by 30% by the end of the month. Dad and mom, please, discuss with them. They're excellent workers. Mbaya, would you like to say something?" Caleb asked.

"I would like to emphasize that the workers at the cows are very conscientious about their work. Also, I would like to thank dad, mom, and Caleb for allowing me to share my knowledge about cows with all who needed to know it," Mbaya said.

"You are very welcome. You, Caleb, and the workers at the cows have done us proud. Let's clap for you because of the great work you did at the cows," The Pastor said.

After clapping, Caleb's mom stood up and prayed:

"We thank our heavenly Father for bringing Mbaya into our life. Through Mbaya, you've given us very insightful lessons on how we can look after our cows for greater benefits. You've also given us conscientious workers. We pray for your blessings upon them and their families. As our children prepare to go to school next week, we pray that their minds will be attuned to school work so that they can excel in all they do. We pray for Mbaya to find good friends and do well in his new school. We pray in Jesus name."

Everybody said, Amen.

The following day, the Pastor took Caleb and Mbaya for lunch at the Farmers Restaurant in town.

"It is said that a change is as good as a rest. That's why I brought you here for lunch. What will you eat and drink?" The Pastor asked.

"Grilled chicken, fries, day's vegetables, and a Sprite for us," Caleb replied.

"Is that so, Mbaya?" Yes dad.

"What will you have sir?" the waiter asked the Pastor.

"Tomato and lettuce sandwich and a cup of hot tea," The pastor said.

As they ate lunch, the Pastor asked Mbaya whether he would mind if his parents were contacted to tell them about him.

"I don't want to see my parents until I'm finished with school. I have a mental problem concerning them. Please, don't contact them for now. It will affect my school performance," Mbaya said.

"I understand your problem. Well, as an appreciation for your good work, I want to buy a gift for each of you. What would you like me to buy for you?" The Pastor asked.

"Dad, that is very kind of you," Caleb and Mbaya said in unison.

Caleb and Mbaya consulted for a while.

"Please, buy a pair of black shoes and socks for each of us," Caleb replied.

"Is that all you need to go back to school?" The Pastor asked.

"No, dad. Mbaya will need a box to put his belongings. He doesn't have one," Caleb said.

"Fine. You will also need new shirts, pants, underwears as well as personal care items, such as, dental cream and soap." the Pastor said.

"Thank you dad for your understanding and generosity," Caleb and Mbaya said.

After lunch, the Pastor led Caleb and Mbaya to a store next to the Farmers Restaurant. The store was large and divided into various departments. Caleb and Mbaya picked up carts for putting their shopping and headed to the shoes section. After searching in the shelves for a while, each picked up the correct size of black shoes with corresponding socks.

"Look over there. The sign reads men's clothing," the Pastor said.

At the men's clothing section were small cubicles, some for men and some for ladies. Caleb and Mbaya picked up various sizes of shirts, pants, under wears, and entered one cubicle. They wore various sizes of shirts and pants, removed them again and again, until they obtained the correct sizes of pants and shirts. At the personal care items, they picked up four tubes of dental cream and four bars of bathing soap. As they pushed their carts along the store's isles, they came across a shelf full various colors of boxes.

"Hey, Mbaya! Don't forget to pick up a box for your clothes and other items," the Pastor said.

"Thank you, dad," Mbaya said.

Mbaya and Caleb went to the shelf and chose a blue box similar in size to Caleb's.

Highly elated, Caleb and Mbaya hugged the Pastor and thanked him profusely for the day.

Caleb and Mbaya Go to School

On Monday the following week, the Pastor drove Caleb and Mbaya to school. The school was ten miles away from the Pastor's home. It was in a suburb and on a fifty-acre land. The school was built near the middle of the fifty acres. On its periphery was a fence of cedar posts that were fixed at five feet intervals. The fence was also secured with thick barbed wire that made the fence almost impenetrable. To the west of the compound was the main gate whose color was black. The gate was twenty feet wide and ten feet high manned by a security guard. At the top of it was written in large letters "JUNIORS AND SENIORS ACADEMY (JSA)." To the east and south of the school compound were smaller gates that led to the teachers' houses. In the northern part of the school compound were soccer, hockey, volley ball, tennis, and athletics fields. Because it was summer, the grass in the fields was brown, and, in some cases the grass had completely dried up.

In middle of the school compound were two huge buildings between which was a smaller building. One of the huge buildings housed classrooms for the primary school while the second one housed classrooms for the secondary school. The smaller building consisted of the Principal's office, teachers' staffroom, and offices for various clerical staff. Two dormitories were situated to the east of the compound.

They entered the Principal's office at 2 p.m. The Principal's secretary welcomed and gave them seats.

"Please, wait," the secretary said and went into the Principal's office.

"You may go in now," the secretary said.

"How are you Pastor? I see you've two students," the Principal

said.

"I'm very well, thank you. This is Caleb, my son. He's is joining grade seven this year," the Pastor told the Principal.

"Of course, I know Caleb. Welcome back. I wish you the best this year. As you know next year will be your final year," the Principal said looking at Caleb.

"Thank you, sir. I will be prepared for it," Caleb replied.

"Great! Who is the other boy?" the Principal asked.

"This is Mbaya Zungu. He comes from CRC Rehab. He did so well at CRC Rehab that he was given a scholarship for his grade three class. Here is the CRC's letter and scholarship papers," the Pastor handed over the documents to the Principal.

"This is a great letter. The scholarship papers are also good," the Principal said.

"Mbaya Zungu, welcome to Juniors and Seniors Academy (JSA). Feel at home and make good friends," the Principal said.

"Thank you sir, I will do my best," Mbaya replied.

The Principal asked his secretary to escort Caleb and Mbaya to their respective dormitories. She made sure that they got uniforms, other personal care items, and were comfortable in the dormitories.

"I'd like to make a special request, Mr. Principal. Any issues concerning Mbaya while in this school, contact me instead of his parents. The relationship with his parents isn't good. That's why he lives with us," the Pastor told the Principal

"That's okay with me," the Principal replied.

Before going home, the Pastor went to see Caleb and Mbaya. He bade them goodbye and went home.

Caleb took Mbaya around the dormitories and introduced him to other students including dormitory prefects. Caleb's introductions of Mbaya, coupled with Mbaya's previous dormitory experience at the CRC Rehab, enabled Mbaya to settle down very well at JSA. The following day, Mbaya attended grade three class. To his amazement, Stadi, his former friend and companion at CRC Rehab was in the same class. Before either Mbaya or Stadi could talk to each other, the class teacher arrived.

"Good morning, students?" the teacher said.

"Good morning Madam," the students replied.

The class teacher laid on her table a list of student names in that class.

"When I call out your name, stand up and say, 'Present'," the teacher told the students.

Out of the twenty students registered for grade three, nineteen were present.

"Most of you were in this school last year. But, I notice that two students are new. You will need to introduce yourself to the class by standing up and telling the class something about yourself, such as, your name, where you come from, your previous school, and what you want to be in the future. Is it that clear?" the teacher asked.

"Yes Madam," the students replied.

One by one students introduced themselves. More time of introduction was given to the two new students.

"You two came from CRC Rehab?" the teacher asked.

"Yes Madam," replied Mbaya and Stadi.

"Did you know that you would come to JSA before you left CRC Rehab?" the teacher asked.

"No Madam. All we knew was that we had scholarships to help us attend any school of our choice," Mbaya and Stadi replied.

"Welcome! I wish you the best in this school," the teacher said.

One by one, each of the other seventeen students stood up and warmly shook hands with Mbaya and Stadi.

"Well, let's turn to your daily program for this semester. Every day, except Saturday and Sunday, your program will start at 6.00 a.m. and end at 9.00 p.m. when you go to bed. Make sure you understand when each activity starts and ends. Saturday after breakfast, is a cleanup day of both inside and outside the dormitory until 11.30 a.m. On Sunday, Church is at 9.00 a.m. to 10.00 a.m. Every body is free thereafter. However, on Saturdays and Sundays, there is a roll call at 4.30 p.m. to ascertain that all students are present. Any questions about the semester program?" the teacher asked.

Many students raised up their hands to ask questions.

"Yes Madam. Please, allow us to study the program and ask questions tomorrow," Mbaya said.

"Class, do you agree with Mbaya's suggestion? If you do, raise up your hand," the teacher asked.

All the students raised up their hands.

The following day, the teacher supplied students with class textbooks and stationery and then asked, "Before we go any further, do you have any questions?"

"Yes, Madam. Is English grammar and English short stories done in the same period?" one student asked.

"That's a great question. No, they will be done on alternate days. That is, English grammar will be done, say, today and English short

161

stories the following day. The same thing will apply to music and art," the teacher answered.

"My question is about the semester program. Are we allowed to go to town on Saturdays and Sundays after lunch?" Stadi asked.

"Yes. But you must register with your dormitory prefect before you go out of the school compound. Ensure you don't get involved in illegal activities out there, and, remember the roll call at 4.30 p.m.," the teacher answered.

"When are parents or guardians allowed to visit their children?" Mbaya asked.

"That's an excellent question. Parents and guardians are allowed to see their children one Saturday a month. Each student must register with the dormitory prefect which Saturday their parent/guardian will visit them," the teacher answered.

The teacher and the students developed a good rapport for the rest of the semester. During break that morning, Mbaya and Stadi met to discuss their future in Juniors and Seniors Academy.

"Oh man, it's good to see you again!" Stadi said as he hugged Mbaya.

"I thought you would go to another school far away. This is great. We're together again!" Mbaya replied.

Caleb Advises Mbaya and Stadi

As Mbaya and Stadi planned their future at JSA, Caleb joined them.

"Hi Caleb! Do you remember Stadi?" Mbaya asked.

"Oh yes. You were together at CRC Rehab. How are you doing?" Caleb asked.

"We are doing very well. Our teacher is good and encouraging. We want to plan and work as a team," Mbaya told Caleb.

"That's great. Contact me if you need my help" Caleb said.

"Can you meet with us on Saturday after lunch in the common room?" Mbaya asked.

"Yes, I'll meet with you but not in the common room. We'll meet in my dormitory. I'm a prefect and I've been assigned a cubicle where it's more private," Caleb answered.

"Fair enough. We'll meet in your cubicle on Saturday after lunch," Mbaya and Stadi said.

They dispersed. Mbaya and Stadi went for a science class while Caleb went for a math class. During the week, Mbaya and Stadi enjoyed class work and playing soccer and hockey games.

"How is the week going?" Caleb asked Mbaya and Stadi.

"Great," Mbaya and Stadi replied.

"Do you remember our meeting scheduled for today in my cubicle?" Caleb asked Mbaya and Stadi.

"Yes, we're looking forward to it since lunch is over," they answered.

"Welcome to my cubicle," Caleb told Mbaya and Stadi.

"Stadi, have a seat on the only chair I have. Mbaya and I will sit on my bed. This is my seventh year here at JSA. It is important for you to obey your dormitory prefects. They have a lot of discretion in decision making. Also, be outstanding in your academic work and games. Every year, students in all dormitories compete in games and sports and academics. Individual students that excel in these activities are given trophies and scholarships," Caleb said.

"Wow, what an incentive to work hard!" Mbaya said.

"This is a good reason for us to work as a team. We did the same at CRC Rehab and our performance was stellar. That's why CRC Rehab gave us scholarships to come to this school," Stadi said.

"Good! Do the same or better here at JSA. If you encounter a problem, don't hesitate to contact me for assistance," Caleb said.

It was Saturday afternoon and Mbaya and Stadi had signed to go to Downtown city. They asked Caleb to accompany them and he agreed. Downtown city was two miles away from school. The road from school to Downtown city was well paved with pedestrian pavements on both sides.

"Look at those trees on both sides of the road. They have beautiful purple flowers," Mbaya said.

"Do you know the name of the trees?" Caleb asked.

"No, this is the first time I have seen them," Mbaya replied

"And me too," Stadi said.

"These are jacaranda trees and they produce flowers in this season," Caleb said.

"The air here is refreshing and the flowers make the place beautiful," Stadi commented.

"You are correct but within a few months, the flowers and the leaves will be shed. All the trees will look dry," Caleb explained to Mbaya and Stadi.

As Caleb, Mbaya, and Stadi approached the city center, there was too much noise from the honking of public service vehicles and the touts.

"Let's go into a restaurant and have some refreshments. I know you're thirsty but not so hungry?" Caleb said.

"I'll drink a cold coke and eat one doughnut," Mbaya said.

"And me too," Stadi said.

"I'll drink a sprite and eat a doughnut," Caleb said.

As they were eating and drinking Mbaya asked, "What time is it?"

"It's 3.30 p.m.," Caleb replied.

"We better hurry up. We don't want to be late for the school roll call at 4.30 p.m.," Mbaya said.

They ate doughnuts and drank sodas hurriedly, walked back to school, and reached on time for the roll call.

During the games session the following Monday, the games tutor selected Mbaya and Stadi to join soccer and hockey school teams. Both had exhibited expertise in playing soccer and hockey since joining the school.

"Which position do you play in soccer?" the games tutor asked Mbaya.

"I'm a left wing striker," Mbaya said.

"And you, Stadi?" the games tutor asked.

"I'm a center forward," Stadi said.

"I want you to know that we shall be playing soccer against Downtown Academy (DTA) in a month's time. We will have soccer practices every day of the week. Do you have any questions or comments?" the games tutor asked.

"Shall we go to Downtown Academy (DTA) or will they come here?" Stadi asked.

"They will come to our school. As there're no more questions, you're are dismissed for today," the games tutor said.

Excitedly, Mbaya and Stadi ran toward the dormitories to shower.

"This is really great. We will win that soccer match against DTA," Stadi told Mbaya.

"I feel so," Mbaya answered.

The First Soccer Match in High School

On the day of the soccer match, DTA arrived at JSA two hours earlier than scheduled. The DTA soccer team wore red uniforms while J and S Academy team wore blue uniforms. At 3.00 p.m., the whistle was blown and the match started. Encouraging loud cheers from supporters of both teams to score goals filled the air. Nonetheless, soccer playing was concentrated on JSA side of the field. After fifteen minutes, the soccer ball was kicked toward the goalkeeper of JSA. The goal keeper jumped up with hands raised to catch it but the ball passed below his left hand to hit the net behind him. It was a goal! As the match continued, Mbaya hit the ball out of the field near the JSA goal posts. It became a corner kick. A DTA player hit the ball so strongly that the JSA goal keeper was unable to stop it. The first half of the match ended with two to zero goals in favor of DTA team.

When the second half of the match started, Mbaya got the ball and passed it to Stadi. As a center forward striker, Stadi dribbled the ball across the field and hit it directly toward the DTA goalkeeper. The ball passed between the goalkeeper's legs and hit the net behind him. There were loud cheers for Stadi. Thereafter, DTA players seemed to congregate around Stadi to stop him from scoring another goal. Mbaya, as a left wing striker got the ball, struck it to pass over the goalkeeper's head to hit the net behind him. There was a standing ovation for Mbaya by the JSA spectators. The DTA team started playing defensively to stop SJA team from scoring more goals. They started kicking the ball up in the air instead of passing it to one another. Mbaya quickly took the ball, dribbled it around DTA players near him and struck it right through the goal posts. He scored a second goal. There were shouts of joy from JSA spectators and boos from DTA side. It was ten minutes before the final whistle to end the match. Soccer ball playing was concentrated on the DTA side. One player kicked the ball into the air over Stadi's head. Stadi headed the ball past the goalkeeper to the net. The JSA spectators stood up, clapped and shouted "Goal! Goal!" Meanwhile, the soccer tournament ended. It was four to two goals in favor of the JSA team. Mbaya and Stadi were lifted up and carried shoulder high by members of their team, JSA. They were the heroes of the day.

The following Monday, Mbaya and Stadi were in the English grammar class. The Principal's secretary popped in the class and requested that Mbaya and Stadi accompany her to the Principal's office. With fear and trembling, they unquestionably followed her.

"How are you doing, young men?" the Principal asked.

"We are fine, sir," Mbaya and Stadi replied.

"I want to congratulate both of you for making it possible for JSA to win the soccer match last Saturday. It's the first time this school won a soccer match against DTA team. How do you feel after this great achievement?" the Principal asked.

"Mbaya and I feel enormously encouraged," Stadi replied.

"We started working together as a team since we were at CRC Rehab and intend to do the same here," Mbaya said.

"That's very insightful. Reports from your teachers show that you are tops in every class," the Principal said.

"Thank you, sir. We didn't know that aspect of our school work," Mbaya and Stadi said.

"That's why you were asked to come to my office to be informed of your progress. Also, I wish to tell you, Stadi, that you will be the soccer captain of the primary school team. And you,

Mbaya, will be the assistant soccer captain of the same team. The games tutor will give you more details later. Okay?" the Principal asked.

Beaming with excitement and feeling overwhelmed by the good news, Mbaya and Stadi said, "Yes sir."

"Excellent! You may now go back to class," the Principal said.

Mbaya and Stadi went back to their English grammar class only to find that the teacher had dismissed it. They went to math class. When the math class ended, it was break time. Students congregated around bulletin boards outside classrooms reading announcements from the Principal's office. It was a congratulatory message to both Stadi and Mbaya for their great soccer performance and elevation to soccer captain and assistant captain respectively.

"Wow! Wow! This is unbelievable! We don't usually get announcements like this from the Principal's office," one student said.

"Think about it. We came to JSA four years ago. Has JSA won a single soccer match against DTA?" another student asked.

"No. Definitely Stadi and Mbaya deserve recognition. They scored four goals for JSA versus two goals scored by DTA," a third student said.

Several students shook hands with Mbaya and Stadi and congratulated them for their extra-ordinary achievement for the school. Some students, who had been in the school longer than Mbaya and Stadi were jealous. Nonetheless, Mbaya and Stadi continued to work together and to excel in their classes and soccer. In grades four, five, six, seven, and eight, the soccer team played eight matches under the leadership of Stadi and Mbaya as captain and assistant captain respectively. JSA won five matches and DTA won three matches.

High School Preparation

To go to high school, students in grade eight had to pass a national examination with a minimum of grade "B" in every subject. After Mbaya and Stadi did grade eight national examination, the school closed for the year end vacation.

"We worked so hard for the national examination but my feeling is that I didn't do well. What about you?" Mbaya asked Stadi.

"Well, I'm not sure how I did but I think the examination was fair. There was nothing outside what we learned in class," Stadi replied.

"You are correct. But, I hope to earn good grades to go to high school. I don't have any other plans," Mbaya said.

"And me too. Don't you think JSA has been good for us?" Stadi asked Mbaya.

"It has been great. Our achievements in class and soccer were recognized. My hope is that our examination grades will be good enough for admission in the JSA high school section," Mbaya replied.

"Team work has helped us a great deal," Stadi said.

"Of course, since CRC Rehab days," Mbaya said.

"Bye-bye for now. I hope we'll meet again soon," Stadi said.

"I hope so also and see you soon," Mbaya replied.

After Christmas holidays, Mbaya receive a letter from JSA. He asked his friend, Caleb to open and read it aloud to him.

"Listen up, Mbaya! You did very well in your national

examination. You achieved four straight "As" in math, science, GHC (Geography, History, Civics), and arts and music. In English composition you achieved a "B+" and in English grammar a "B." Congratulations!" Caleb said.

Mbaya breathed a sigh of relief.

"Thank you very much, Caleb. I thought I had flunked in English grammar and composition. What a relief!" Mbaya said.

"And, that's not all from the letter," Caleb told Mbaya.

"What else does the letter contain? Please, read it out," Mbaya asked.

"Your good performance in the examination and in school, earned you a grant to pay for all your high school education, board and tuition. How about that?" Caleb said.

"It's beyond my expectations," Mbaya replied.

"The letter also says that you report at school on time. 'Congratulations!' and the letter ends," Caleb said.

"Thank you. Now I'm happy and encouraged because my future looks bright," Mbaya said.

"Going to College is now within your grasp. However, you will need to work hard in high school to compete for the few positions that are available at university," Caleb told Mbaya.

Mbaya in High School

Paul, Caleb's older brother, took Mbaya to high school in JSA as was scheduled. Mbaya reported his arrival and signed his name on a register in the admission office. A school officer, in-charge of admission directed Mbaya to his dormitory.

"Are you Mbaya?" the dormitory prefect asked.

"Yes, I am," Mbaya replied.

"Welcome to our dormitory," the prefect said.

The prefect showed Mbaya his bed. His supplies, such as, blankets, towels, school uniform were placed on his bed.

"Wear the uniform, and, if it doesn't fit you, bring it to me and I'll issue you with another one, Okay?" the prefect asked.

"Okay," Mbaya replied.

The school uniform fitted Mbaya very well. After making his bed, Mbaya went to see the dormitory prefect.

"See, the uniform is a perfect fit," Mbaya told the dormitory prefect.

"That's great," the prefect said.

"By the way, do you know whether my friend, Stadi was admitted in this school?" Mbaya asked.

"Do you mean the former primary school soccer captain?" the dormitory prefect asked.

"Yes, yes," Mbaya replied.

"No," the dormitory prefect replied.

"What might have happened to Stadi? May be he went to

another high school," Mbaya thought.

During supper, the teacher on duty asked all new students to stand up to be welcomed. Former students clapped three times to welcome them. Also, every new student stood up, introduced himself and named his dormitory. Mbaya and Stadi recognized each other during the introductions.

"What a relief to see you!" Mbaya told Stadi.

"And me too!" Stadi replied.

After supper, Mbaya and Stadi, hugged each other warmly and moved to the school's common room. They sat at a corner of the common room where few other students noticed them.

"Have you noticed that we have ten subjects to study in the next four years?" Stadi asked.

"Yes, they are: English language, English literature, Math, chemistry, physics, biology, geography, history, and commercial studies. We also need to study and pass one other language such as Kiswahili, French, German, or Spanish," Mbaya said.

"You may choose to study six to 10 subjects including English and math for the final examination," Stadi said.

"Since the national examination will be done in grade 12, the final year in high school, we have time to consider what to do in the finals," Mbaya said.

"I think by the end of our second year, we will be able to decide which subjects to do in the finals. What do you think?" Stadi asked.

"I think so. We will have gained enough experience since the content of each subject becomes more and more complex every year. Meanwhile, let's start meeting after supper to discuss our progress or challenges and what to do about them," Mbaya replied.

"Agreed," Stadi said.

Mbaya and Stadi shook hands and went to their respective dormitories. The following day, the games tutor approached Mbaya and Stadi.

"It is no secret that both of you are great soccer players. Your reputation has spread among soccer players within the school and other schools outside. Would you mind joining high school soccer team?" the games tutor asked.

"We would be happy to join it," Mbaya and Stadi replied.

"That's great! Remember that soccer practices take place on Fridays from 3 p.m. to 4 p.m.," games tutor said.

"That's okay with us," Mbaya and Stadi answered.

"Hey Mbaya! Would you like to continue playing as a left wing striker?" the games tutor asked.

"Yes sir. I don't want to change," Mbaya replied.

"And you Stadi?" the games tutor asked.

"No change sir. I will continue to play as a center forward," Stadi replied.

"Bye-bye. See you tomorrow during soccer practice," the games tutor said.

As they went away toward their dormitories, Stadi saw a bulletin board near the soccer field.

"Hey Mbaya look! This is a list of all soccer players in the high school section," Stadi said.

Stadi and Mbaya drew closer to the bulletin board to peruse the soccer players' list. Of the twenty-two soccer players, only three were selected from their fresh man's class.

"That's great honor bestowed on us, to be in the first soccer team during our freshman's year," Stadi said.

"True, but it's going to be hard work for us. As you know, I'm struggling in chemistry, physics, and biology lab work. It means spending a lot of time in the lab," Mbaya said.

"I'm also struggling in history. I have to read the text many times to remember the dates. It also means we have to ask many questions from our teachers while in class and continue our team work," Stadi said.

During their freshman's year in high school at JSA, the soccer team played against two high school visiting teams. Mbaya and Stadi scored two goals each out of the eight scored against the visiting teams. This helped the school maintain its leading position in soccer among the neighboring high schools. In contrast, Mbaya and Stadi found that high school academic work was more challenging than they expected.

"My year end academic report shows that I haven't flunked in any subject. I have two straight "As" in math and commerce, two "Bs" in French and English language and "Cs" in all other subjects. The report is worse than I expected. What about you?" Mbaya asked.

"Like you, I didn't flunk in any subject. I earned six straight "As" and two "Cs" in Commerce and French respectively. We need to improve our grades," Stadi said.

"That's great, Stadi. I feel we should give up some of the physical activities, such as soccer or hockey and concentrate on our class work in order to improve the grades," Mbaya said.

"You are correct, Mbaya. However, I think we should continue to assess our academic performance more regularly, say, each time we do a quiz or an examination. If we find no improvement, we take action," Stadi answered.

During third and fourth years in high school, Mbaya gave up soccer. By the middle of the fourth year, his grades started to improve. Stadi's grades remained steady and he continued to play soccer and led the soccer team as captain. When they did the national high school examination at the end of the fourth year, Mbaya scored three straight "As," four "Bs," and one "C" in Biology. Stadi scored six straight "As," and two "Bs" in French and commerce respectively. Mbaya and Stadi were admitted to different universities. Mbaya went on to study accounting and Stadi to study medicine aiming to become a heart surgeon.

Mbaya's Life before University

Mbaya returned to the Pastor's home after high school. The Pastor's children had all completed university education and were working in different careers. While at the Pastor's home waiting to go to university, he had a dream that kept nagging him for days. The dream reminded him of his earlier encounter with Kogi while drawing water, and, how he injured him on the way home from school.

"Will Kogi accept my apologies after so many years? How shall I approach him? Did he go on with education as I did?" Mbaya questioned himself.

"What is on your mind, Mbaya? You look greatly disturbed," the Pastor asked.

"I had a dream which continues to nag me every day," Mbaya replied.

"What was the dream about?" The Pastor asked.

"It was about Kogi, the boy I bullied one morning while drawing water, and, injured him as we went home from school," Mbaya replied.

"I know all about it from his father and the community elders. What do you intend to do about it?" the Pastor asked.

"I don't know since it's been such a long time. Please, advise me," Mbaya replied.

"For your information, Kogi did very well in the national high school examination. He scored eight straight "As." He has been admitted at the same university to which you will be going," the Pastor told Mbaya.

"I would like to meet him in your presence. Is that possible?"

Mbaya asked.

"I don't know, but I can try. Do you mind the presence of your dad, Kogi's dad, the chief, and other village elders?" the Pastor asked.

"No. I'd like to meet them also," Mbaya replied.

The Pastor contacted the chief of Mbaya's area to arrange for a meeting between Kogi and Mbaya. Kogi's father, Kubwa, and Mbaya's father, Zungu were also invited. On the meeting day, Mr. Kubwa was accompanied by Kogi and two other village elders, and, Mr. Zungu by his wife. The meeting started at 10.00 in the morning.

"Ladies and gentlemen, this meeting has been called by the Pastor. The purpose of the meeting is to try to reconcile Mbaya and Kogi. You all know what happened between them twelve years ago. First, I want to congratulate both of them for their stellar performance in the national examination. It is now your responsibility and mine as well, to ensure that Kogi and Mbaya are reconciled. This will make them be positive contributors in our community. With that introduction, the Pastor takes over the running of the meeting," the chief said.

"Thank you, chief. I'm glad you all agreed to attend this meeting. In case you don't know, Kogi and Mbaya are admitted at the same university. I would also like you to know that Mbaya requested this meeting to apologize to Kogi. Without further delay, I call upon Mbaya to say what is on his mind," the Pastor said.

"I want to thank the Pastor for all he has done and continues to do for me. Additionally, I'm indebted to you, chief, and the community elders for sending me to CRC Rehab eleven years ago. I'm a better human being because of it. There is a Scripture that says, 'Forgive us the wrongs we have done, as we forgive the wrongs that others have done to us,' (Matthew 6: 11, TEV). I have regularly asked God to forgive me for my past misdeeds to my former classmate, Kogi. Will you, Kogi, forgive me for bullying and hurting you twelve years ago?" Mbaya pleaded.

"I still have psychological problems when I remember the way you thrust me into the river as I drew water for my grandmother. My left foot bears this huge scar because of the injury you inflicted on me as we went home from school. Consequently, my natural instinct is not to forgive you. However, the story of Joseph in Genesis 50: 15–21 became very compelling to me. Joseph forgave his brothers after a long time since they almost killed him before they sold him to be a slave in Egypt. Just like it took time for Joseph to forgive his brothers, it will take time for me to forgive you." Kogi replied.

"Thank you all the same, Kogi. I'm terribly sorry for what I did to you," Mbaya replied.

The meeting ended after two hours after which the Pastor and Mbaya went back home. Neither Mbaya nor his parents talked to each other during or after the meeting.

Mbaya and his Parents meet Kogi's Father

Two weeks after Mbaya met Kogi, his parents and Kogi's father visited him. The Pastor had consulted Mbaya to invite them to discuss his future. Kogi's father, Kubwa, came in his capacity as the chairman of the elders' committee in their community.

"Welcome to our home. This is my wife and between us, we have four children who are working after finishing their university education. The purpose of this meeting is to let you know what Mbaya has done since he left home twelve years ago. I think, there is no other better way to inform you about it than Mbaya telling it himself. Mbaya, get on with it," the Pastor said.

"I left home as a prisoner after leading a gang of boys who terrorized and stole things at night from our community. I had stopped going to school but lied to my parents that I was still in school. What made me become a gang leader and lie to my parents?" Mbaya asked.

"Answer that question for us. You had a good home, good food, all you needed for school, and, I think we were good Christian parents and teachers," Mbaya's father, Zungu, replied.

"As a teenager, I had many questions which neither you, my parents, nor my teachers helped to answer," Mbaya said.

"Give examples of the questions we didn't answer as your parents," Mbaya's father asked.

"I respect you as my biological parents. However, you forced us as kids to behave in ways that were very ordered and no questions were entertained from us. Also, you didn't provide time to discuss teenage problems which were many. As my father, you were unapproachable and I feared you. Consequently, I joined a group of boys who had similar problems to look for answers,"

Mbaya said.

"I'm glad you respect us as your parents. The book of Ephesians chapter 6 verses one to three says, 'Children, it is your duty to obey your parents, for this is the right thing to do.' 'Respect your father and mother' is the first commandment that has a promise added: 'so that all may go well with you, and you may live a long time in the land,' (Ephesians 6: 1-3, TEV). This was our motivation in bringing you up," Mbaya's father replied.

"Allow me to say something in this discussion, Mr. Zungu. You've quoted a very pertinent and accurate section of the Bible. However, verse four of the same chapter says, 'Parents, do not treat your children in such a way as to make them angry. Instead, bring them up with Christian discipline and instruction,' (Ephesians 6: 4, TEV). As a father, I know how easy it is to discipline our children and forget to instruct them. Instruction occurs when we correct mistakes that they make and when we listen to them," the Pastor said.

"I think instruction also means that we should allow our children to express themselves freely in our presence. This allows us to seize teaching moments and correct any errors they make, and, also learn from them," Mr. Kubwa, Kogi's father said.

"What the Pastor and Kogi's father said explains it aptly. I also didn't feel loved because my parents imposed on me rules that were unreasonable and arbitrary. In spite of working hard and doing my chores, I never pleased them. When I went to CRC Rehab, I was counseled, my work was appreciated, made friends, and did great to get a scholarship. This Pastor and his family became instrumental to my progress in school. They loved and encouraged me to do my best. Additionally, they are a model of a Christian family in relation to dealing with children. They are my family," Mbaya told his biological parents.

"Have you disowned us as your parents?" Mbaya's father asked.

"You are still my biological parents though you neglected to bring me up as your own child," Mbaya said.

"Mbaya, you know you're our third child. You started rebelling against us before going to school. One Scripture says, 'Teach a child how he should live, and he will remember it all his life,' (Proverbs 22: 6, TEV). That's why we decided to discipline you so that you may behave better and have a fulfilling future," Mbaya's father said.

"If I may, I'd like to say a few words concerning what Mr. Zungu has said about Mbaya. Mr. Zungu seems to use the same method to discipline different errant children. Because of differences in children's behavior, each child should be treated differently because each is unique. When Mbaya's parents noticed his unique behavior, they should have acted in love to help him out of it. I also think that biblical verses should be interpreted wisely bearing in mind their past and present cultural contexts," Mr. Kubwa said.

"I disagree with Mr. Kubwa. He and other village elders have conspired to destroy my family. They made it difficult for Mbaya to come home after he was released from CRC Rehab," Mr. Zungu said.

"Oh, no, no, father, Mr. Kubwa wanted me to come home. But my mother refused because my presence at home would have worsened your illness," Mbaya told his father.

"What Mbaya has said is true. It happened during the first meeting we had with the chief, the elders, and Mbaya's mother. You, Mr. Zungu couldn't come because you were ill," the Pastor said.

"Mr. Zungu, we have been helping you build up your family, not destroy it. If Mbaya didn't go to the CRC Rehab, he would have been jailed or killed if he continued as a gang leader. He is the first of your children to go to university and his future looks great. How does this make you conclude that the elders, led by me, have conspired to destroy your family?" Mr. Kubwa, the elders' chairman, asked.

Looking exasperated by what Mr. Kubwa said, Mr. Zungu, Mbaya's father, stood up, beckoned his wife, and, both stormed out of the room and went home.

Who stole the money

Mbaya and Kogi met again and seemed to be good friends while studying at the same university. Mbaya majored in accounting and Kogi in marketing. After finishing their studies, both were employed by the same firm headed by Caleb, an old friend of Mbaya. Kogi always wore a clean grey suit whose color matched his shoes and tie. He always wore a cheerful smile that endeared him to his juniors and seniors. Though at times unpopular with the creditors, he did very well in credit control and money collection

Mbaya, unlike Kogi, wore a dark brown suit whose color clashed with that of his shoes and tie. His smile was always sardonic and rough. However, he was meticulous as a financial accountant and was endeared by cashiers who worked under him.

One day, Kogi came to the office at 6.00 p.m. from a credit collection trip. Mbaya was still in the office trying to balance figures in his financial budget.

"Mbaya, my office is locked. Would you, please, keep this money for banking tomorrow?" Kogi asked.

"No problem, bring it in. However, make sure you collect it tomorrow morning and give it to the cashier because I shall be on vacation," Mbaya told Kogi.

Mbaya was on vacation when he received a letter from his supervisor asking him to report back at work. He went to see the supervisor. Although the supervisor pretended to be friendly, Mbaya noticed some uneasiness and reservation from the supervisor's behavior toward him. Mbaya realized that something sinister had occurred in his department.

"What happened between you and Kogi the evening before you went on vacation?" the supervisor asked Mbaya.

"Kogi came to my office at 6.00 p.m. and requested me to keep the money he had collected that day. I also told him to collect the money and give it to the cahier for banking the following morning," Mbaya told his supervisor.

"Did you count the money?" the supervisor asked.

"No, sir, because I trusted him," Mbaya replied.

"You are now in great trouble because there was no burglary and the money was missing the morning you went on vacation. Kogi says it was $30,000, which included cash and cheques. Everything else was intact. Your finger prints were the only ones recognized by the police," the supervisor told Mbaya.

Mbaya was dumbfounded.

"Who would have stolen the money? Could the cashier have stolen it? Could Kogi, my friend, have made a duplicate key secretly? What will happen to my wedding preparations with Jane that I had gone on vacation to arrange?" Mbaya's mind was clouded with these questions.

Mbaya's friends were of the opinion that somebody else but Kogi had stolen the money.

Mbaya went to court to defend himself against the accusation that he stole the money. Although he had employed a famous attorney, his fingerprints implicated him so much that he lost the case. He was imprisoned for two years on account of theft. Despite his imprisonment, Mbaya's conscience was clear that he did not steal the money. And, though he was not a committed Christian, Mbaya prayed day and night that God may one day vindicate him.

Eight months after Mbaya's imprisonment, Jane, his former fiancee and Kogi visited him in prison. Both tried to convince him that the cashier had stolen the money, but they didn't have any tangible evidence to help Mbaya.

One day while in prison, Mbaya listened to a very inspiring sermon from the prison chaplain. It was about God's goodness to those who suffer many troubles from the evil people of this world. The sermon emphasized how God would protect and save his people, (Psalms 34: 19 -22, TEV). His perception of the world was drastically changed. It became the turning point in Mbaya's life as he prayed more fervently to God to reveal the person who stole the money. Instead of feeling a sense of self-pity for his imprisonment, loss of a job, and loss of a fiancee, Mbaya experienced a peace of mind hitherto unknown to him. He became more obedient to the prison warders and the prison became like a home to him. He made many friends among the prison warders and the prison inmates. News of Mbaya's changed life spread like wild fire in his former workplace and at his home.

One morning, Mbaya had his breakfast of half-cooked and inadequate porridge. Before Mbaya and the other prisoners went to work in the prison garden, the head warder called out, "Mbaya, come to the gate immediately!"

"How are you, Mbaya?" two men asked him in a chorus.

"I'm fine except for being in prison," Mbaya replied.

Meanwhile, the two men took out two parcels, one for Mbaya and the other for the prison warder. They contained well grilled beef and French fries wrapped in brown paper. Like two hungry wolves, Mbaya and the prison warder gobbled the food and thanked the two friends profusely after eating.

"Do you remember the day Kogi left the money in your office before you went on vacation?" one of the men asked Mbaya.

"Yes, I do," Mbaya replied.

"That day, Kogi had knocked and killed a man while driving. Kogi needed money to bribe a policeman so that the accident wouldn't be followed up by the police. He took the money from your office the evening you left to go on vacation," the visitor informed Mbaya and the prison warder.

"That evening, Mbaya wrote a letter to Jane, his former fiancee but Jane didn't reply to that letter. A few months later, Mbaya was released from prison.

When Mbaya went home, he learned that Jane was married to Kogi. A week later, Jane and Kogi came to see Mbaya at his apartment. They invited him for supper at their house.

Mbaya pondered and wondered whether or not to go for that supper.

"Come on in Mbaya, and feel at home. Both Jane and I were concerned about your prison sentence but we were unable to avert it," Kogi said after receiving Mbaya for supper.

After dinner, Jane asked Mbaya, "Who stole the money from your office?"

There was complete silence for twenty minutes and one could hear a pin drop. Then, Mbaya, looking at Kogi and smiling broadly replied to Jane, "Ask your dear husband."

Life after Prison

After his release from prison, Mbaya lived alone in his apartment trying to adjust himself to life out of prison. One Sunday, he decided to attend church closest to where he lived. The ushers were very friendly. One of the ushers handed him a brochure containing the order of the church service, and, led him to a seat in the middle of the sactuary. A prayer was said by a church elder, two hymns were sung followed by announcements.

"We welcome you all to this morning church service. We especially extend a special welcome to those who are here for the first time. Please, put up your hands if this is your first time here. Thanks. May I also request that you stand up, tell us your name, your career, and where you come from," the announcer said.

Mbaya stood up. "My name is Mbaya. I'm a committed Christian and a financial accountant. I live in this neighborhood but right now I don't have a job because I was recently released from prison after wrongful imprisonment."

After Mbaya, other visitors stood up and introduced themselves. What was exceptional was that the visitors came from different countries of the world.

"Thank you all, and, note that all our visitors are welcome to tea, coffee, and snacks in the church hall after this service. Please, stand up to sing the hymn 'Amazing Grace' as shown on the brochure," the announcer said.

After singing the hymn "Amazing Grace," a tall gentleman in a blue suit and a matching tie moved up to the pulpit. In a baritone, he read the Scripture in Jeremiah 29: 4-14 (TEV), prayed and preached. He talked about the story of the children of Israel exiled in Babylon. They were without hope and were deceived by false

189

prophets who lived among them. Through Jeremiah, God told them not to listen to the false prophets but to stay in Babylon. After seventy years, God would bring them back to their home in Israel. The plans God had for them were for prosperity, not for disaster, and, he would bring a future they hoped for. This would make them pray and seek God wholeheartedly and they would find him.

"Well, well, Jeremiah 29:4-14 (TEV) is so relevant to my life. My stay in prison was like the exile of the children of Israel in Babylon. I also listened to many philosophies propounded by their adheherents while in prison that were similar to the false prophets. I thank God for the prison chaplain God used to challenge me accept Jesus as the Lord and master of my life. I do not know what the future holds but I believe that God promises a good future not a bad one," Mbaya thought.

As tea, coffee, and snacks were being served in the church hall, a number of people approached Mbaya to emphathize with him because of his past imprisonment. Two chief executive officers from multinational consulting firms gave Mbaya their business cards. Each one of them asked Mbaya to report to their offices the following week. As they were leaving the church hall, a lady approached Mbaya.

"Hey! I think we've met before. It was nice to hear you introduce yourself in church today. My name is Koe," the lady said.

"Thanks Koe but do you care to remind me where we met?" Mbaya asked.

"Do you remember your former boss?" Koe asked.

"Do you mean Caleb?" Mbaya asked.

"Correct. I'm his secretary," Koe replied.

"Wow! Wow! This is incredible! Praise the Lord!" Mbaya said.

"Do you mind if I talk to Caleb about you tomorrow?" Koe asked Mbaya.

"Not at all," Mbaya replied.

The following Monday at 10.00 a.m., there was a knock at Mbaya's apartment door. After looking through the door's keyhole, he opened the door.

"I'm Caleb's driver. Are you Mr. Mbaya?" the driver asked.

"Yes," Mbaya answered.

"Caleb asked me to take you to his office before 11.00 a.m. today," the driver said.

"Okay, give me ten minutes to prepare myself," Mbaya replied.

At 11.00 a.m., Mbaya was in Caleb's office.

"Good morning Mbaya?" Koe said.

"Good morning. It's nice to see you again," Mbaya said.

Koe led Mbaya into Caleb's office. The office had a clean, light blue wall-to-wall carpet. In the middle of the office was a well polished semi-circular mahogany desk and Caleb sat on large blue colored executive chair. There were four other smaller chairs around Caleb's mahogany desk. Caleb was reading a financial magazine when Koe and Mbaya entered his office.

"Hello brother Mbaya. It's been such a long time since we met. I'm delighted that Koe persuaded you to come to see me. How are you doing?" Caleb asked.

"I'm doing as well as I can in my present circumstances. The Lord has been great to me," Mbaya replied.

"By the way, dad and mom send their warm regards to you. They are eager to see you and discuss things. When is the best time for you to see them?" Caleb asked.

"Any day when they are free," Mbaya replied.

"Will next Sunday at 2 p.m. be appropriate?" Caleb asked.

"Sure. It will be appropriate," replied Mbaya.

"Thanks. My driver will pick you up from your apartment at 1.15 p.m. next Sunday," Caleb said.

"Fair enough. I'll be ready at that time," Mbaya responded.

"Koe told me you don't have a job yet. Would you mind coming back to work in our company again?" Caleb asked.

"I wouldn't mind. However, it would be beneficial for the company and myself if I were exonerated from the theft case for which I was sent to prison," Mbaya replied.

"I understand what you mean. We know you didn't steal the money. The only evidence the police had was your finger prints found where the money was kept in your office. As far as the company is concerned, you are innocent. Moreover, insurance paid for the stolen money," Caleb told Mbaya.

"Thank you for that explanation. How will you deal with employees' perception that I stole the money?" Mbaya asked.

Caleb looked at Mbaya for a few seconds and said, "Our lawyers will write a letter to exonerate you. The letter will be distributed to all employees in the company and to you as well," Caleb told Mbaya.

"That sounds great," Mbaya said.

"Good. Let me know after ten days whether or not you want your job back as a financial accountant," Caleb told Mbaya.

The following morning, Mbaya went to see one of the CEOs who gave him a business card at church the previous Sunday.

"Good morning Mr. Mbaya?" the CEO said.

"Good morning sir," Mbaya replied.

"Have a seat and feel comfortable. Would you like a cup of coffee or tea?" the CEO asked Mbaya.

"Tea, please," Mbaya replied.

Mbaya was drinking tea when the CEO explained the origins of his company, and, its global reach as a financial consulting corporation. The CEO indicated that there was a vacancy for a financial accountant for which he thought Mbaya would be suited. The organizational chart on the wall showed that after one year of probation, the financial accountant would be elevated to the position of financial director of the corporation's branch.

"Are you interested in being our finanacial accountant?' the CEO asked.

"Yes, sir," Mbaya replied.

"Very well. Would you mind to explain why you were imprisoned as you mentioned on Sunday at church?" the CEO asked.

"Yes, sir. One evening, a credit controller came to the office late in the evening carrying $30,000 collected from customers. The cashier had gone home. He kept the money in my office to give to the cashier the following morning. He knew I was going on vacation the following day. While on vacation, my supervisor called me back to the office who revealed to me that the $30,000 had been stolen. I was shocked. My finger prints were the only evidence that incriminated me as the one who stole the money. My lawyers tried hard to defend me but in vain. So, I was sent to jail for two years," Mbaya explained.

"I'm so sorry about it. I'm glad you came out from jail earlier than two years," the CEO said.

"While in jail, I prayed to God to reveal the person who stole the money from my office the night I went on vacation. I also became a committed Christian after the prison chaplain preached a sermon on Psalms 34: 19-22 (TEV). This scripture says that those who believe in God will suffer from evil people of this world. The scripture also says that God would protect and save his people from the evil people. I was encouraged to pray harder," Mbaya said.

"Praise the Lord! Tell me more," the CEO asked.

"Eight months later, two friends from the company I worked for came to see me in jail. They brought me food I hadn't eaten for months. They also revealed to me that a colleague stole the money from my office. He needed the money for paying policemen to avoid incrimination in a car accident he had caused," Mbaya narrated.

"Thank you for your candidness. I think I have made my decision. Come here on Wednesday morning next week and bring copies of your degrees. Do you have any questions?" the CEO asked.

"No sir," Mbaya replied.

"Fair enough. Have a good week and see you next week," the CEO told Mbaya.

Mbaya was excited, humbled, and couldn't restrain himself from reciting in his heart, "The Lord is my shepherd; I have everything I need, He lets me rest in fields of green grass and leads to quiet pools of fresh water," (Psalm 23:1-2, TEV). That night Mbaya knelt beside his bed and prayed, "Thank you, Almighty God, for the two job offers made to me this week. Please, show me where you would best use me for your glory. In Jesus name I pray, Amen."

"At 1.45 p.m. the following Sunday, Caleb's driver picked Mbaya up from his apartment and brought him to Caleb parents' home. It was more than six years since Mbaya contacted Caleb's parents, the Pastor and his wife.

"Well! Well! What a great day this is, to see Mbaya again! Welcome home and have a seat," the Pastor said.

Before Mbaya sat down, Caleb's parents hugged him fondly patting him at the back. Meanwhile, Caleb, his wife, and Koe, his secretary arrived. After the exchange of greetings between Caleb, his wife, Koe and Caleb's parents, Caleb's dad, the Pastor, prayed for the buffet lunch set before them.

"Oh God our heavenly father, we thank you for good health, friends and family and for gathering us here today. We thank you for Mbaya who went through trying circumstances and is here with us. We thank you for the food set before us to eat. Lord, we ask for blessings on many people who have nothing to eat. Bless our fellowship together and all that we say, think, and do may bring honor and glory to your name. This we ask in the name of Jesus. Amen," the prayer ended.

After lunch, everybody moved to the lounge where tea and coffee were being served.

"I'm so grateful to see Mbaya and Koe who haven't been in our home for a while. Mbaya is our son and we welcome him back," Caleb's mom said.

"I'm delighted to be back home, and, sorry I couln't visit you earlier than today. As you know, after university, Kogi and I were employed by the company for which Caleb and Koe work. One late evening, company's money that Kogi left in my office was stolen. My fingerprints found by the police implicated me in the theft. I was sent to prison for two years because of the money I hadn't stolen. But one Sunday morning while in prison, the chaplain told us that a good person may suffer many troubles but the Lord saves him from them all. Those who go to the Lord for protection will be spared (Psalm 34:19-22). After that sermon, I became restless and went forward for counseling. I accepted the Lord as the master of my life. I had peace and joy and started to pray that the Lord may vindicate me and get me out of prison. I was released from prison after eight months," Mbaya narrated.

The Pastor and his wife stood up. Caleb, his wife, and Koe stood up as well. All of them shouted, "Hallelujah! Hallelujah! Hallelujah!" as they hugged Mbaya.

"Thank you very much," Mbaya said.

"What are your immediate needs, Mbaya?" the Pastor asked.

"Right now I need a job before considering other life's issues. Caleb and Koe have been very supportive in this respect. In addition, I got a job offer from a church member I met a week ago when I met Koe. He is a CEO of an international financial consulting firm. I would be employed as a financial accountant and be elevated to financial director after one year's successful probation. What is your advice?" Mbaya asked.

"Has Caleb promised you a job in their company?" Caleb's mom asked.

"Yes," Mbaya replied.

"In that case, we will join you in prayer for God to show you where you would best serve him," the Pastor said.

"If God leads you to work for the international financial consulting firm, we will be okay. If you are led to work for our company, we will be delighted," Caleb told Mbaya.

"Thank you very much brother Caleb," Mbaya replied.

Mbaya got a ride to his apartment from Koe. During the ride, Koe persuaded Mbaya to consider taking the job at the international financial consulting firm. The new job had more prospects for advancing his career. Both of them agreed to pray about it. The following week, Mbaya started working for the new company, the international financial consulting firm.

Coming to Terms with Present and Past

Mbaya worked so hard at his new job that after one year of probation, he was promoted to financial director. He developed excellent rapport with his supervisors as well as his juniors. The sky seemed to be the limit in his career advancement. Meanwhile, his relationship with Koe blossomed.

"I have enjoyed your company and the sharing of ideas every time we are together. I feel peaceful and fulfilled," Mbaya told Koe.

"And me too since we met at our church for the first time," Koe told Mbaya.

"May I suggest something?" Mbaya asked Koe.

"Yes, of course," Koe replied.

"As Christians, we need to be transparent in our relationship to prevent gossip and slander. Let's call a fellowship and declare our intentions," Mbaya said.

"Wow! That is great. Where would we have the fellowship?' Koe asked.

"At Caleb parents' home," Mbaya replied.

"Why not at our church?" Koe asked.

"That would be a great altenative. However, the Pastor and his wife are like my parents. They took me in their home since rehab in grade two right up to university," Mbaya replied.

"In that case, I agree with your suggestion. Should we invite our parents?" Koe asked.

"Of course, you may invite your parents. I also think that we should tell your parents about our relationship in advance of the fellowship. We shouldn't take them by surprise," Mbaya replied.

That weekend, Mbaya and Koe drove to Koe's parents' home. Koe's parents were retired high school teachers. Like Koe, their other three children were working after finishing university education.

"Good morning mom?" Koe said.

"Good morning, Koe. Welcome and have a seat. Can I make tea for you?" Koe's mom asked.

"I'll help you make tea. Please, get dad so that we can have tea together," Koe requested.

Koe's mom went out to call her husband who was busy cleaning the car. Koe's father came in, cleaned his hands, and joined the others at the lounge.

"Hi dad? This is my friend Mbaya," Koe told her dad.

"How are you, Mr. Mbaya? Welcome to our home," Koe's dad said.

"Thank you. I feel welcome," Mbaya replied.

"What is your profession?" Koe's dad asked.

"I'm a financial accountant," Mbaya replied.

"Are you employed?" Koe's dad asked.

"Yes. I work for international financial consulting corporation," Mbaya replied.

"Thank you. My wife and I are retired high school teachers," Koe's dad said.

"The reason we came to see you is to seek your permission as we plan our future together," Koe told her parents.

"Thank you for honoring us with that request. We are happy for both of you. Keep us informed as you go forward with your plans. But, remember to ask guidance from God about everything you do," Koe's father said.

"Thank you for your generosity and advice," Mbaya told Koe's parents.

Koe and Mbaya drove back to their residences happy that they had blessings to proceed with their future plans.

After work the following day, Mbaya went to see the Pastor and his wife. Both were seated at the lounge discussing the day's happenings.

"Hello Mbaya!" the Pastor and his wife stood up to greet Mbaya.

"Hello dad and mom," Mbaya said.

"We are glad to see you. Have a seat and a cup of tea," the Pastor's wife said.

"Many thanks, mom" Mbaya said.

"How are you doing at your new job?" the Pastor asked.

"I'm glad you ask because I came to inform yo about it. My probation ended four months ago and immediately I was promoted to financial director of the company branch. Additionally, Koe and I want to be engaged so that we can plan our future together," Mbaya replied.

"Praise the Lord! Stand up, hold hands together, and, let's thank the Lord. Our heavenly father, we thank you for the great things you've done for Mbaya. Despite many trials and tribulations, all things have worked together for good. Bless the plans he and Koe are making. We pray in Jesus name. Amen," the Pastor said.

"Thank you very much, dad and mom for the prayers and the concern you have for us. May I make a request?" Mbaya asked.

"Yes, indeed," the Pastor's wife answered.

"Koe and I want to be transparent in our relationship. For this reason, we want to invite a few friends in a fellowship to declare our future intentions. Where do you think we should have the fellowship?" Mbaya asked.

"You would honor us by holding the fellowship here in our house. The Pastor would officiate the fellowship, and, Caleb, would be the master of ceremonies. What do you think, Pastor?" the Pastor's wife asked her husband.

"That's a great suggestion," the pastor answered. "By the way, will you invite your biological parents," the Pastor asked Mbaya.

"As a follower of Jesus Christ, I want to be reconciled to my biological parents. But I don't know how they will react since I haven't had any contact with them for many years. What do you think I should do?" Mbaya asked.

"People change over time. I think the three of us should visit them and find out what's going on. The Pastor can make those arrangements. What do you think?" the Pastor's wife asked her husband.

"Fine," the Pastor replied.

"Thank you. Will you accept a ride in my car to visit my biological parent's home?" Mbaya asked.

"Absolutely, we shall be honored to have a ride in your car," the Pastor answered.

"Thank you. When would it be appropriate for the fellowship to be held without much inconvenience to you?" Mbaya asked.

"Well, well. Let me check my dairy. Two months from now

will be appropriate," the Pastor replied.

"That is good because we'll be able to make the necessary contacts, including a visit to my biological parents," Mbaya said.

One month before the fellowship date, Mbaya went to pick up the Pastor and his wife to visit his biological parents. They arrived at Mr. and Mrs. Zungu's home, Mbaya's parents, just before lunch. The Pastor came out of the car and walked towards the house. Before he reached the house, Mrs. Zungu came out of the house and met the pastor smiling.

"Hello Pastor?" Mrs. Zungu said.

"Hello Mrs. Zungu," the Pastor answered.

After a few minutes of discussion, the Pastor led Mrs. Zungu to the car.

"Who are these visitors you came with?" Mrs. Zungu asked.

"At the back seat is my wife. The driver is your son, Mbaya, and, this his car," the Pastor said.

"I can't believe it. Am I seeing a vision or is it really true?" Mrs. Zungu thought in herself.

Without uttering a word after the introductions, Mrs. Zungu rushed back to the house and came out again accompanied by her husband, Mr. Zungu.

"Good afternoon Pastor? I'm told you've other visitors in the car?" Mr. Zungu asked.

"Yes, Mr. Zungu," the Pastor answered.

"Please, bring them in to the house. It is lunch time," Mr. Zungu said.

After lunch, Mr. Zungu and Mrs. Zungu asked the Pastor the reason for their visit. The Pastor pointed at Mbaya to explain.

"Thank you Pastor. Dad and mom, I left this home as a teenager but now I'm a grown-up man. I know the Lord as my personal savior. We came here today because I need your forgiveness for the wrongs I have done to you. Jesus tells us that if we forgive others for the wrongs they have done to us, our heavenly father will also forgive us. If we don't forgive others for the wrongs they have done to us, our heavenly father will not forgive us for the wrongs we have done, (Matthew 6: 14, TEV). Will you accept me and forgive me?" Mbaya asked his parents.

Nobody spoke for nearly five minutes. Finally, Mrs. Zungu held her husband's hand, pulled him towards Mbaya. Mr. Zungu refused to come near Mbaya or talk to him. Mrs. Zungu said, "I accept you and I forgive you, my son."

"Thank you mom. I also forgive you for all you did or didn't do for me. Additionally, please, know that I have a job as a financial director of an international financial consulting firm. By God's grace, I have found a soul mate. Her name is Koe. Would you like to meet her?" Mbaya asked.

"Yes. Where and when?" Mrs. Zungu asked.

"The fellowship to meet Koe will be in our home in a month's time. It will be on a Sunday evening. We'll fetch you on Saturday afternoon so that you can spend Sunday with us. Will that be okay?" the Pastor asked.

"That sounds good," Mrs. Zungu said.

"By the way, Mom and dad, would you invite Mr. Kubwa, Kogi's dad to come with you for the fellowship?" Mbaya asked.

"We will try to contact him," Mrs. Zungu said.

The Pastor said a prayer to thank God for a meaningful meeting with Mbaya's parents and for a safe journey back home.

After the visit to his parents, Mbaya met Koe to discuss who would be invited to the fellowship. The Pastor would conduct prayers and give a brief talk. His wife would be in charge of catering. Caleb, Koe's boss and Mbaya's best friend would be the master of ceremonies. Kogi and his wife Jane, would be invited as special friends.

"Well… Why invite Kogi and Jane as your special friends?" Koe asked.

"It's a long story. Briefly, I bullied and seriously hurt Kogi when we were teenagers. Jane, his wife, was my fiancée before I was jailed. I feel it's time to harmonize my relationship with Kogi and his wife," Mbaya replied.

"That's great. They are an admirable couple. They have a smart one and half years old son. As you know, Kogi is our marketing director and works very hard to grow our company," Koe said.

"I'm happy for Kogi and Jane," Mbaya replied.

"Hey, how were you received by your parents when you visited them?" Koe asked.

"Mom was stunned to see me and the car. She dashed in to the house and brought my father out. When he came out, he greeted the Pastor but didn't talk to me or the Pastor's wife. After lunch, I asked for their forgiveness. My father refused to forgive me, even to talk to me. Mom forgave me and promised to come to our fellowship," Mbaya replied.

"Thank God your mom was so understanding and welcoming. I think your dad will warm up to us over time," Koe said.

"You see, my father has always been authoritarian. I was amazed that he accompanied mom to see us in the car after we arrived. What was even more surprising was that mom pulled him over to hug me. Of course, he refused," Mbaya said.

"Let's continue to pray and show kindness to him," Koe said.

The fellowship plans for Mbaya, Koe, their parents, and friends were ready. On Saturday evening prior to the fellowship, Mr. and Mrs. Zungu arrived at the Pastor's home. Kogi and his wife, Mr. and Mrs. Kubwa, followed suit as were Mbaya, Koe, Caleb and his wife. Before dinner was served, the Pastor spoke.

"My wife and I welcome you to our home. I want to say a special welcome to Mbaya's and Kogi's parents because this is their second time to visit with us. We are here today and tomorrow because of the two people we love, Mbaya and Koe. They love each other very much. During the fellowship tomorrow evening, they will tell us about their future plans. Let us give thanks to the Lord. Give thanks to the Lord, because he is good; his love is eternal. He did not forget us when we were defeated; his love is eternal; he gives food to every living creature; his love is eternal. Give thanks to the God of heaven; his love is eternal. Amen," (Psalm 36: 1, 23, 25, TEV)."

The following day, the visitors were invited to a worship service at the Pastor's church near his home. A visiting Pastor preached a sermon titled The Power of the Cross. The sermon was based on the words of Jesus on the cross, "Forgive them, Father! They don't know what they are doing," (Luke 23: 34, TEV). The preacher stressed that despite feeling excruciating pain while on the cross, Jesus asked God, the father to forgive the people who instigated, planned, and executed him. Forgiveness opened the way to salvation because we are all sinners, just like those who put Jesus to death. "Everyone has sinned and is far away from God's saving presence. But by the free gift of God's grace all are put right with him through Christ Jesus, who sets them free. God offered him so that by his sacrificial death he should become the means by which people's sins are forgiven through their faith in him. God did this in order to demonstrate that he is righteous,"

(Romans 3: 22-25, TEV). Thus, "God loved the world so much that he gave his only Son, so that everyone who believes in him may not die but have eternal life," (John 3: 16, TEV).

Because God is so loving and gracious, he forgives us and give us new life through his Son, Jesus Christ, and reconciles us to himself. We should also forgive one another and be reconciled in order to have fellowship with one another after the blood of Jesus purifies us from every sin, (1John 1:7, TEV). Broken relationships can hinder our relationship with God. Thus, if we have a problem or grievance with a family member or a friend, we should resolve them as soon as possible because our attitude towards others reflects our relationship with God.

Finally, the preacher told the congregation, "For one minute, I want you to reflect in your heart about any broken relationships you have between you and your family or friends. Ask God to forgive you and give you power to resolve the problem or grievance with those you are involved. Thank God for it. Amen. Go in peace."

At 6.00 p.m. that day, the fellowship started at the Pastor's home. There were twenty people in attendance who were friends and relatives of Mbaya and Koe.

"Good evening everyone. We welcome you to our home and this fellowship dedicated to our loved ones, Koe and Mbaya. Before we proceed, let's give thanks to the Almighty God, our creator. Our heavenly father, we thank you for bringing us together this evening because of love between Koe and Mbaya. We thank you also for the presence of Mbaya's and Kogi's parents who are here with us. We praise you, oh Lord. We pray that all we do, say, and think in this fellowship will be praiseworthy and glorifying to you. We ask all this in the name of Jesus. Amen. I now call upon Caleb to lead the fellowship program," the Pastor said.

"Ladies and gentlemen, it gives great pleasure to talk about two people I know well. I've known Mbaya since he was in grade two. We lived together as brothers in our home. I have seen him grow and blossom, at school, university, and at work. He is very creative, hard working, a good listener, loving, and a great follower of Jesus Christ. I have worked with Koe for the last five years. She is my secretary. She is a follower of Jesus Christ, very innovative, hard working, outgoing, and pleasant to work with. Two years ago, Mbaya attended Koe's church where he gave his testimony during a church service. After the service, Koe contacted Mbaya and their friendship started and blossomed to what we know today. I now call upon Koe to tell us her side of the story." Caleb said.

"Dear parents and friends, I'm glad to inform that it was love at first sight when I met Mbaya at our church two years ago. As he gave his personal testimony, he displyayed sincerity of heart that I had't seen from a man before. We have met many times for lunch at restaurants. In one of those meetings, Mbaya told me how fulfilled he felt every time we met. Surprisingly, that's what I felt when I first met him. Mbaya suggested this fellowship so that we would be transparent to our parents and friends. Thank you for coming. Mbaya, come on and speak," Koe said.

"Thank you Koe for what you've said. I also thank everyone for coming to this fellowship. I extend special thanks to my parents, Mr. and Mrs. Zungu and to Kogi's parents, Mr. and Mrs. Kubwa. They have played special roles in my development as a person. My parents and Kogi's parents, please, stand up. Clap, clap, praise the Lord! We plan our marriage to be on Saturday, December this year, two days before Christmas day. Details will be sent later," Mbaya said and the people clapped.

Mbaya had't finished talking when Mr. Zungu, his father, came forward with his head bowed.

"Brothers and sisters, today is a great day for me and the Zungu family. After church today, I confessed to God the many wrongs I have committed against our son, Mbaya, the rest of my family, and my neighbors. I have been a lukewarm Christian. Many of you may not know that our son, Mbaya, left home many years ago and was brought up by this Pastor, in whose home we are meeting today. Mbaya, my son, will you forgive me for all I did against you, or didn't do for you, as your father?" Mbaya's father asked.

"Yes, father. I forgive you for everything. Will you also forgive me for the pain I caused you in my teenage years?" Mbaya asked his father.

"Yes, my son. I forgive you for everything," Mbaya's father said.

People clapped and sang praises to the Lord as Mbaya and his father were finally reconciled after more than twenty years.

Mbaya's father asked Mr. Kubwa, Kogi's father, to come forward.

"This is our community chairman. I want to thank him publicly for all the work he did towards the rehab of our son, Mbaya. Please, forgive me for the embarrassment and the trouble I caused you on many occasions, in spite of your generous heart and good efforts," Mbaya's father asked.

"I forgive you. It's God who has worked to bring us to this joyous ocassion. We thank him for Mbaya and Koe and pray for their blessed future," Mr. Kubwa said.

After a short interlude, Mbaya asked Kogi to come to the front where he stood.

"For those who don't know, our parents' homes are close to each other. As a frustrated teenager I bullied Kogi by splashing water on him. I also hurt him badly on one of his legs as we went home from school. Kogi, will you, please, forgive me for these bad acts I did against you?" Mbaya asked.

"Sure, I forgive you. I have also done some things indirectly that caused you pain and embarrassment. Please, forgive me and my family. Will you?" Kogi asked.

"I forgive you without any reservation," Mbaya answered.

Everybody in the fellowship stood up, clapped their hands, and sang praises to the Lord as Mbaya hugged his father, Kogi's father hugged Mbaya's father, and Kogi hugged Mbaya. Thereafter, the Pastor said a priestly blessing and dismissed everyone.

CPSIA information can be obtained
at www.ICGtesting.com
Printed in the USA
BVHW030435021222
653276BV00006B/11

9 781953 839459